The Thinking Tree

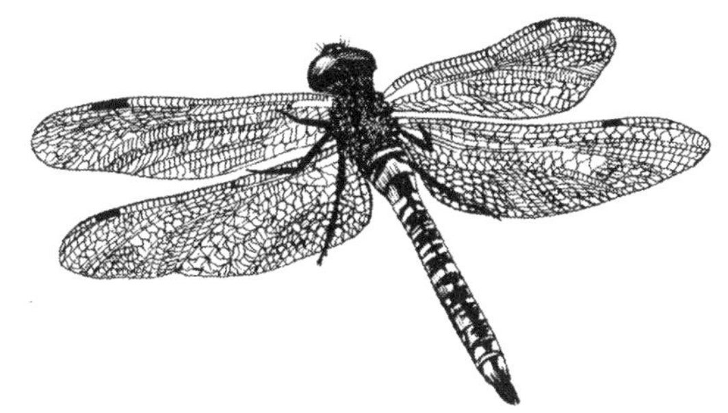

EXPLORING OUR PLANET

EARTH'S NATURAL GEOGRAPHY

Biomes, Landforms & Topography

EARTH SCIENCE, GEOLOGY, ECOLOGY & BIOLOGY

Worldschooling Research Handbook

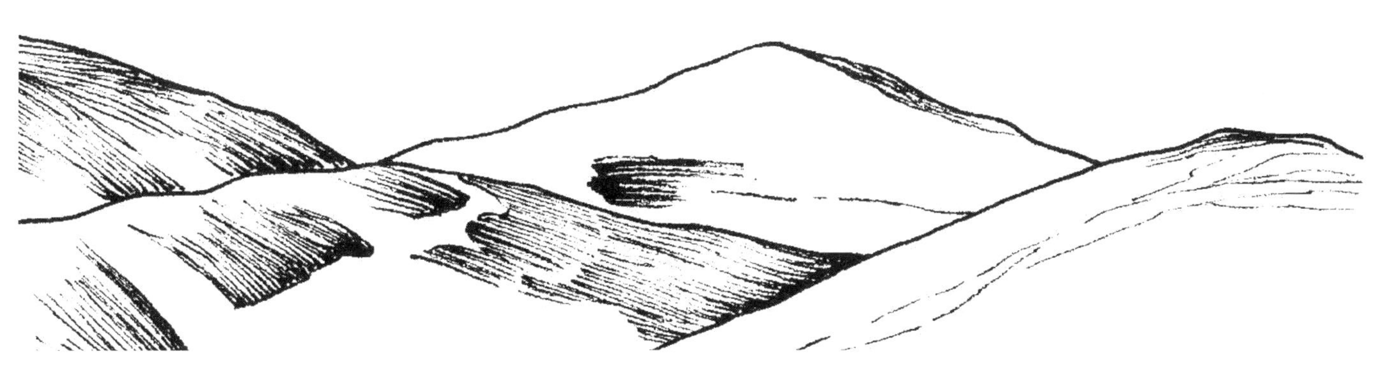

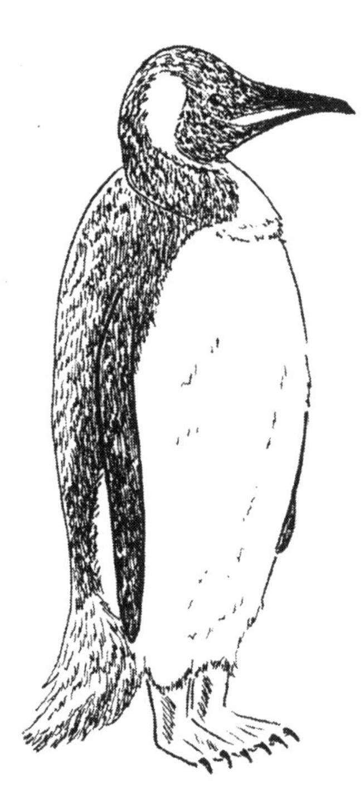

By: Margarita Brown, Anna Kidalova & Sarah Janisse Brown

We use the Dyslexie Font by Christian Boer

The Thinking Tree Publishing Company, LLC

FUNSCHOOLING.COM

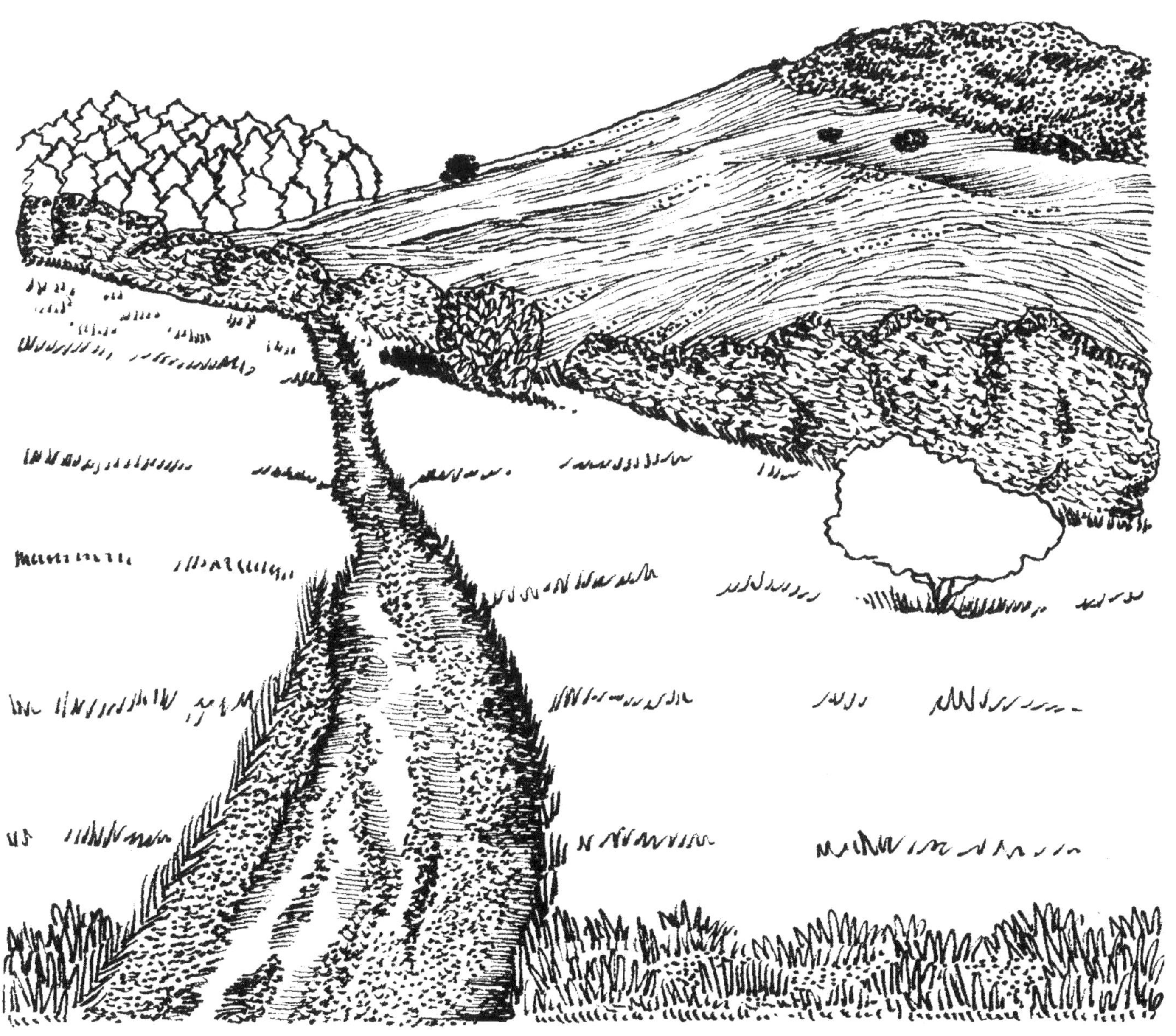

TABLE OF CONTENTS:

ABOUT THIS BOOK:

This research handbook is packed with learning prompts and fun activities that all revolve around the natural features of our planet. The workbook provides 180 pages of learning for of all ages. Studying Earth's natural geography should be fun and full of adventure and creativity. If any of these types of landforms or bodies of water are within a half day's drive, GO! Children ages 9+ should be able to work through this book with minimal assistance, younger children will need help with reading, writing and research. This workbook is fun for all ages, and can be used in collaboration with multiple siblings as a family project. Help your child choose safe research materials and documentaries. Use two pages each day to finish this book in one semester, or use one page a day to make the book last a full school year.

PARENTS PLEASE CREATE A LIST OF APPROVED WEBSITES AND RESOURCES FOR YOUR CHILD:

MY BOOKS

Draw the covers of any books you use in your research:

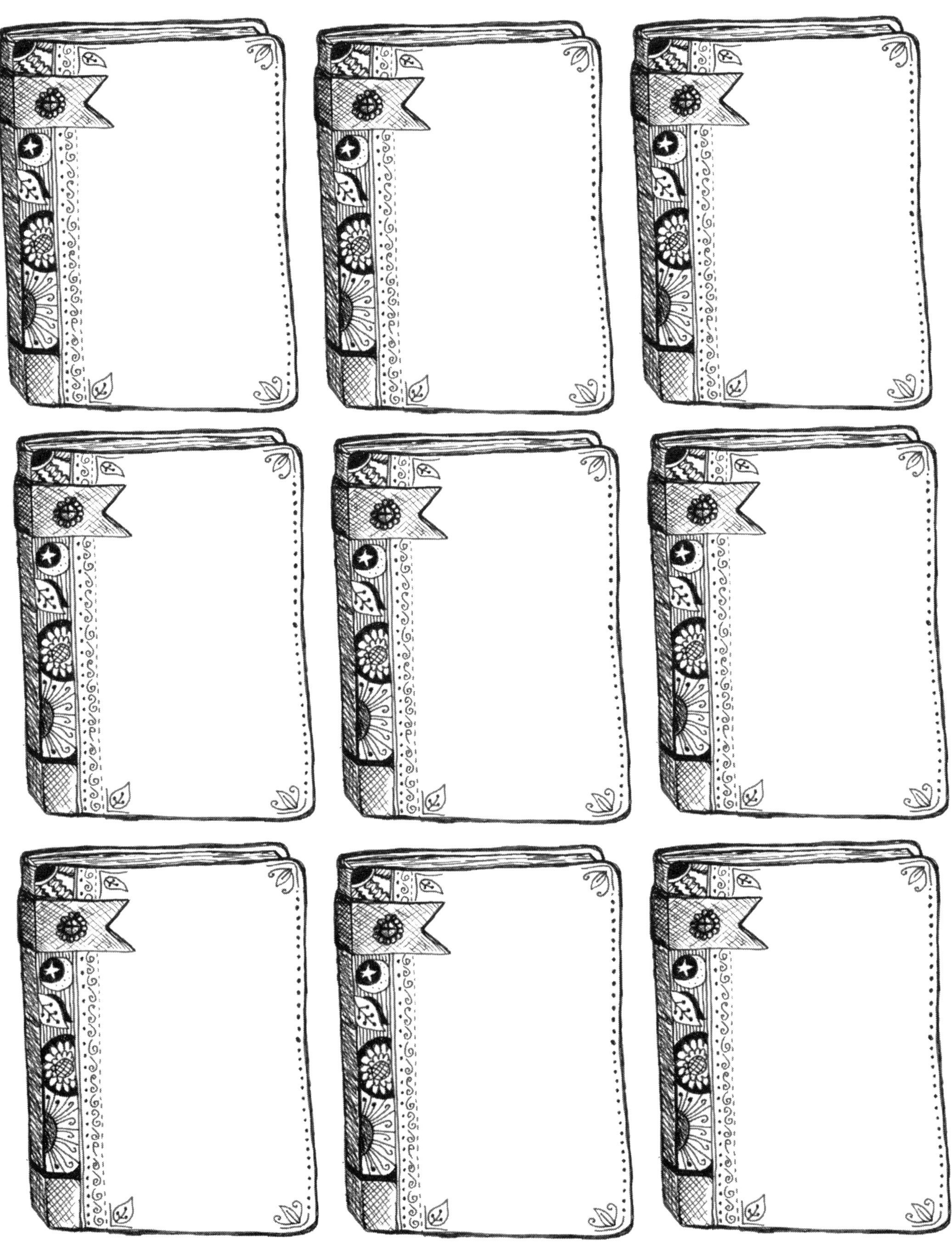

MY LEARNING LIST

Additional Books & Documentaries

TITLE: DATE:

LANDFORMS, BIOMES, AND BODIES OF WATER

Do some research, and answer the questions.

What is a landform?

What are some different types of landforms?

What is a biome?

What are some different types of biomes?

What is a body of water?

What are some different types of bodies of water?

Do some research, and connect the categories to the correct landform, biome, or body of water.

Landform:

Biome:

Body of water:

Other:

Savanna
River
Lake
Ocean
Sea
Waterfall
Forest
Lagoon
Desert
Glacier
Pond
Stream
Canyon
Island
Plateau
Hot spring
Plain
Oasis
Geyser
Rainforest
Volcano
Mountain
Iceberg
Crater
Tundra
Swamp
Valley
Meadow
Hill
Cave
Spring
Quarry

SAVANNAS

Do some research, answer the questions, and write down three facts.

What is a savanna?

Interesting fact about savannas:

What are the different types of savannas?

What kind of climate do savannas have?

Fascinating fact about savannas:

Draw some creatures, plants, and trees that could be found in a savanna.

Do some research, and answer the questions.

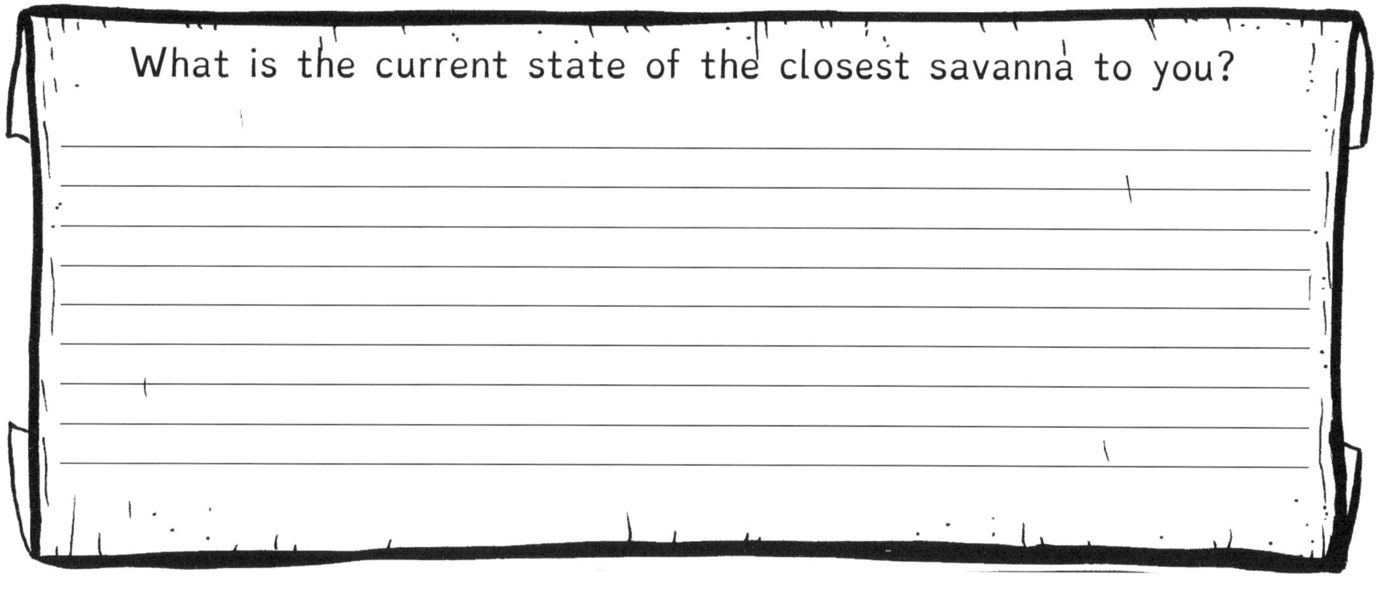

What is the current state of the closest savanna to you?

What kind of influence do people have on this environment?

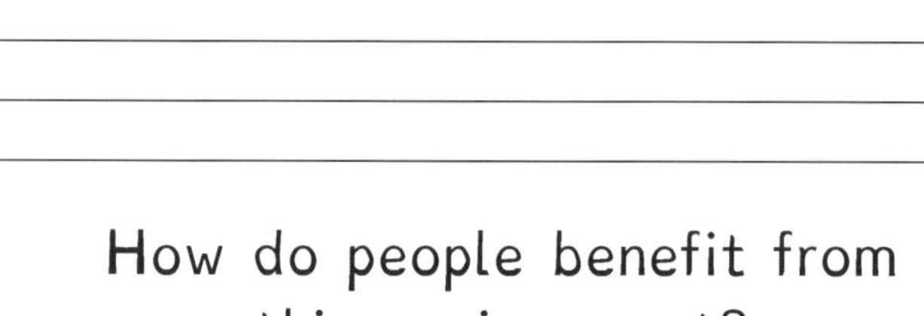

How do people benefit from this environment?

Do some research, and list the top five most well-known savannas in the world. Write a short description for each one.

1. ______________________________

2. ______________________________

3. ______________________________

4. ______________________________

5. ______________________________

Mark on the map the location of each savanna.

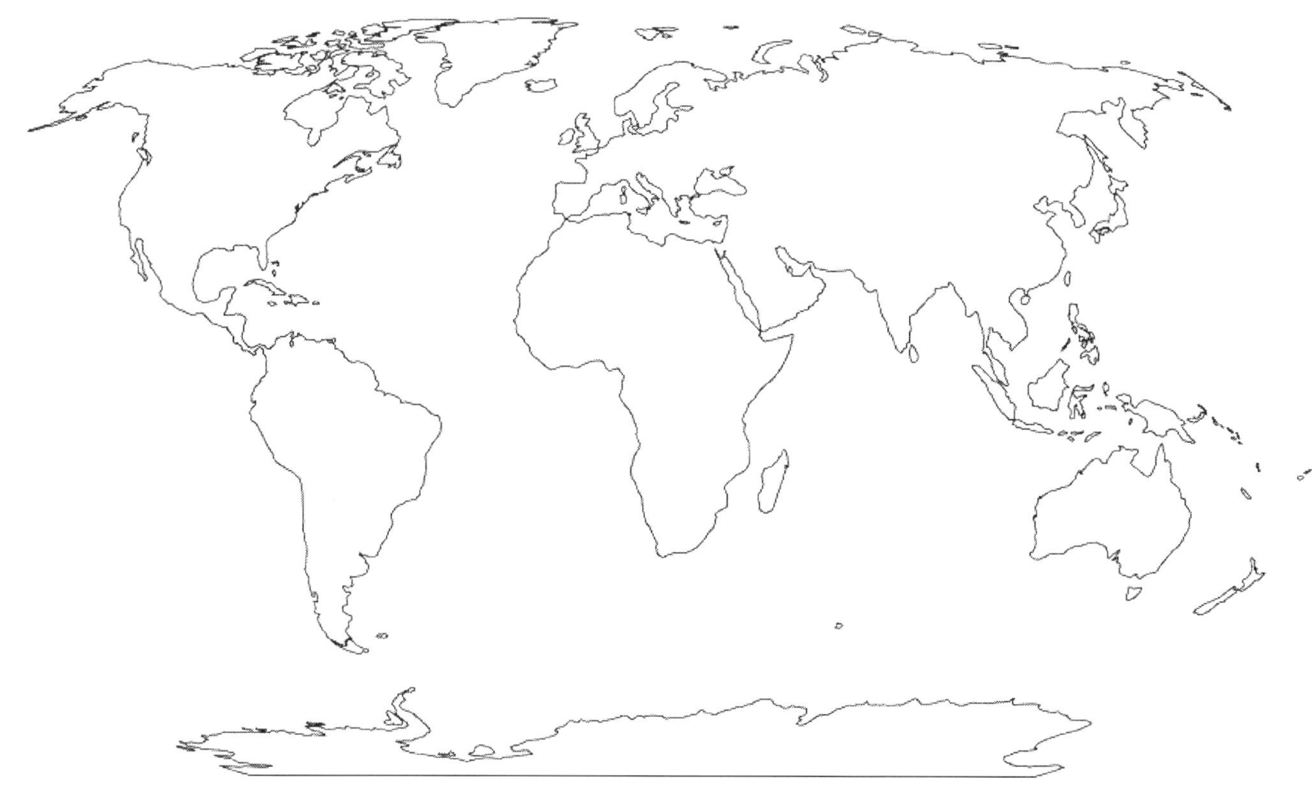

RIVERS

Do some research, answer the questions, and write down three facts.

What is a river?

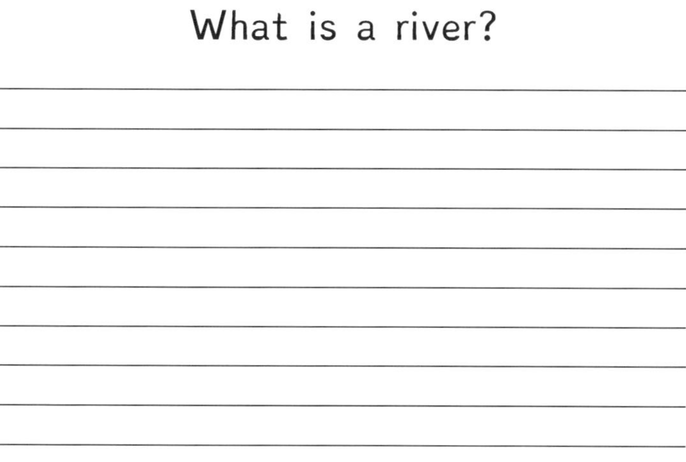

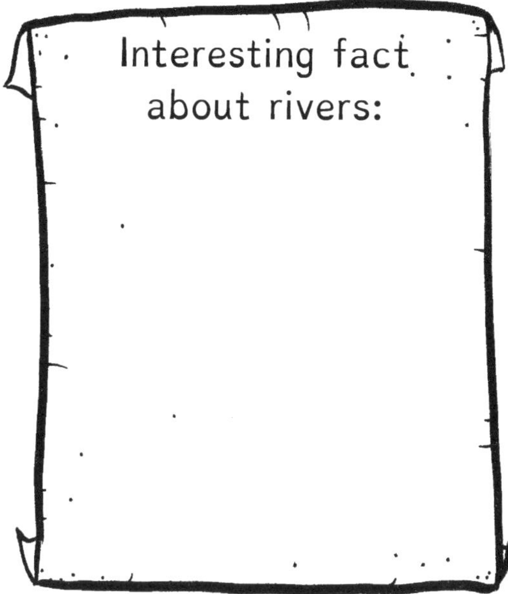

Where does the water in the rivers come from and where does it go?

What is the largest river in the world?

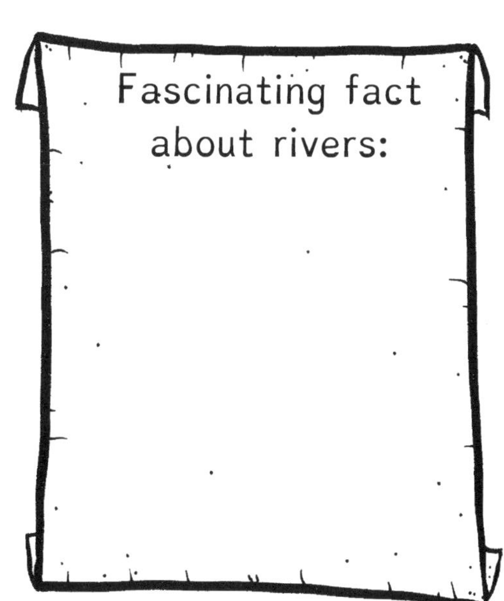

Draw some creatures, plants, and trees that could be found in or around a river.

Do some research, and answer the questions.

What is the current state of the closest river to you?

What kind of influence do people have on this environment?

How do people benefit from this environment?

Do some research, and list the top five most well-known rivers in the world. Write a short description for each one.

1. ______________________________

2. ______________________________

3. ______________________________

4. ______________________________

5. ______________________________

Mark on the map the location of each river.

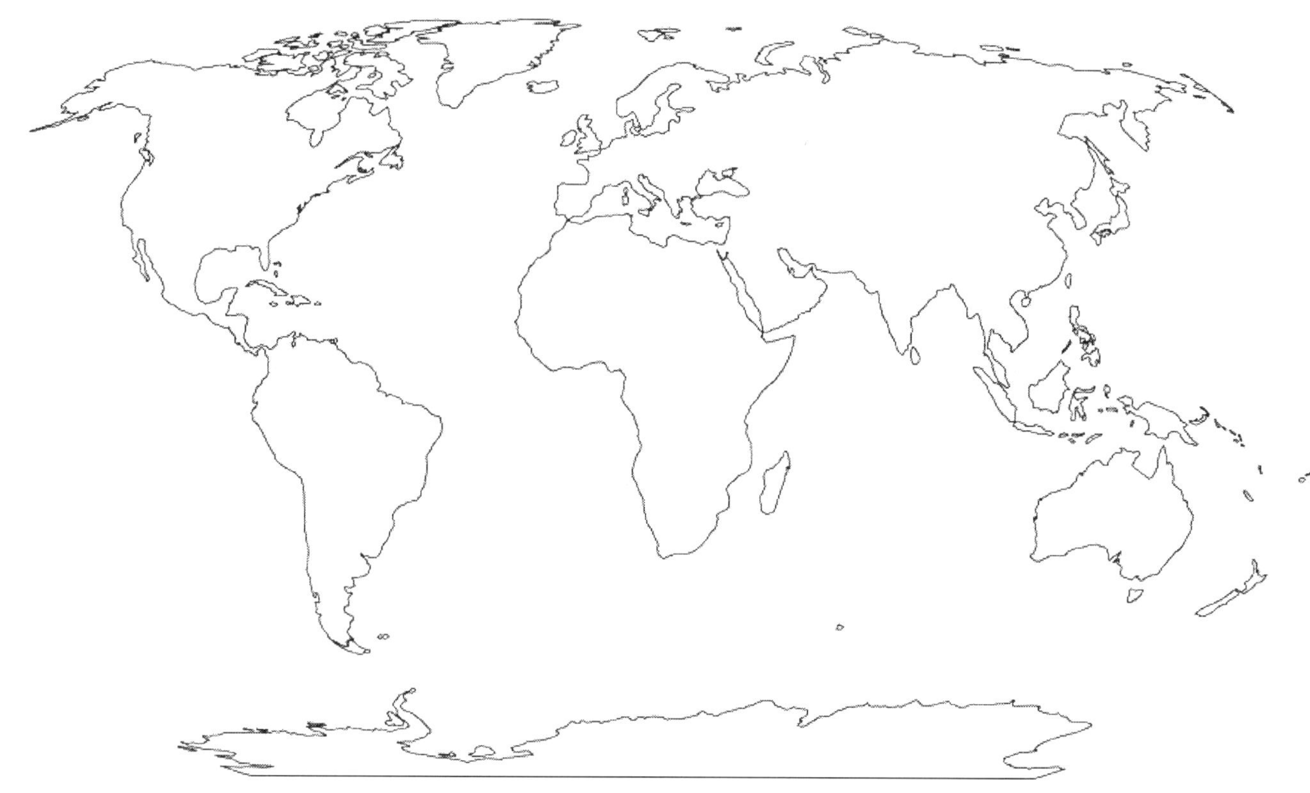

LAKES

Do some research, answer the questions, and write down three facts.

What is a lake?

Interesting fact about lakes:

Fun fact about lakes:

What are the different types of lakes?

What is the largest lake in the world?

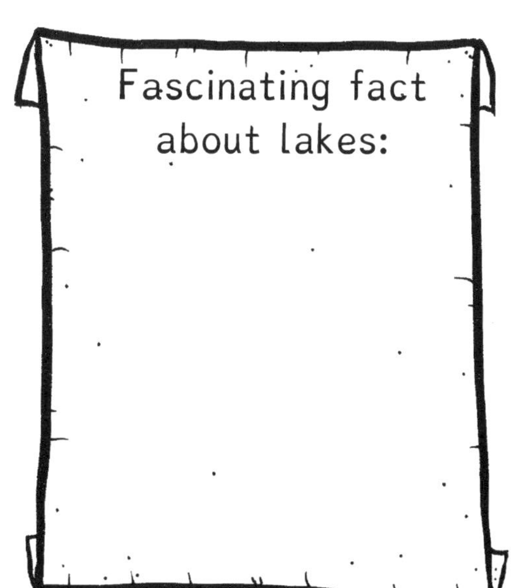

Draw some creatures, plants, and trees that can be found in or around a lake.

Do some research, and answer the questions.

What is the current state of the closest lake to you?

What kind of influence do people have on this environment?

How do people benefit from this environment?

Do some research, and list the top five most well-known lakes in the world. Write a short description for each one.

1. ______________________________

2. ______________________________

3. ______________________________

4. ______________________________

5. ______________________________

Mark on the map the location of each lake.

OCEANS

Do some research, answer the questions, and write down three facts.

What is an ocean?

Interesting fact about oceans:

Fun fact about oceans:

How many oceans are there in the world?

What is the largest ocean in the world?

Fascinating fact about oceans:

Draw some creatures, plants, and trees that could be found in or around an ocean.

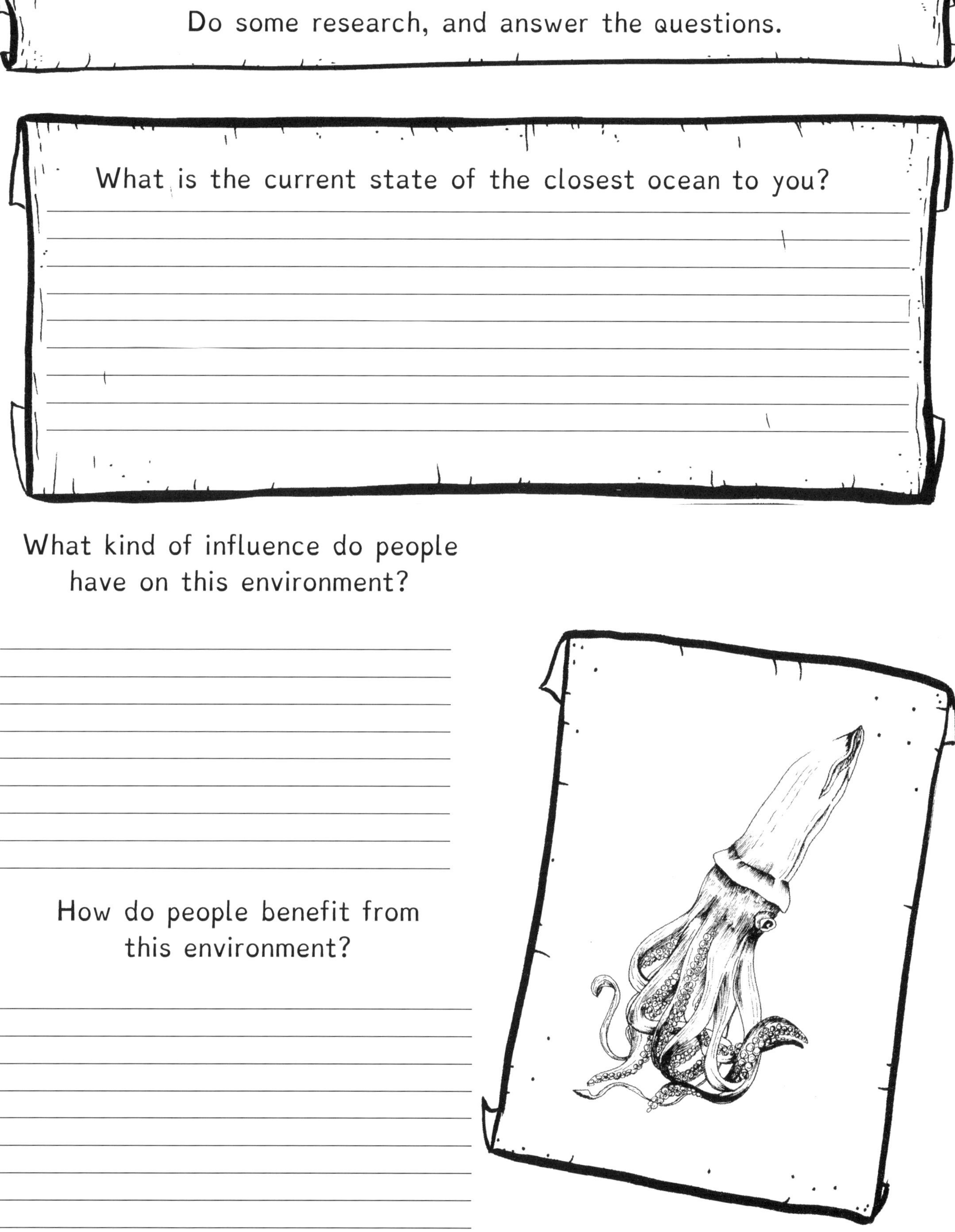

Do some research, and answer the questions.

What is the current state of the closest ocean to you?

What kind of influence do people have on this environment?

How do people benefit from this environment?

Do some research, and list the top five most well-known oceans in the world. Write a short description for each one.

1. ______________________________

2. ______________________________

3. ______________________________

4. ______________________________

5. ______________________________

Mark on the map the location of each ocean.

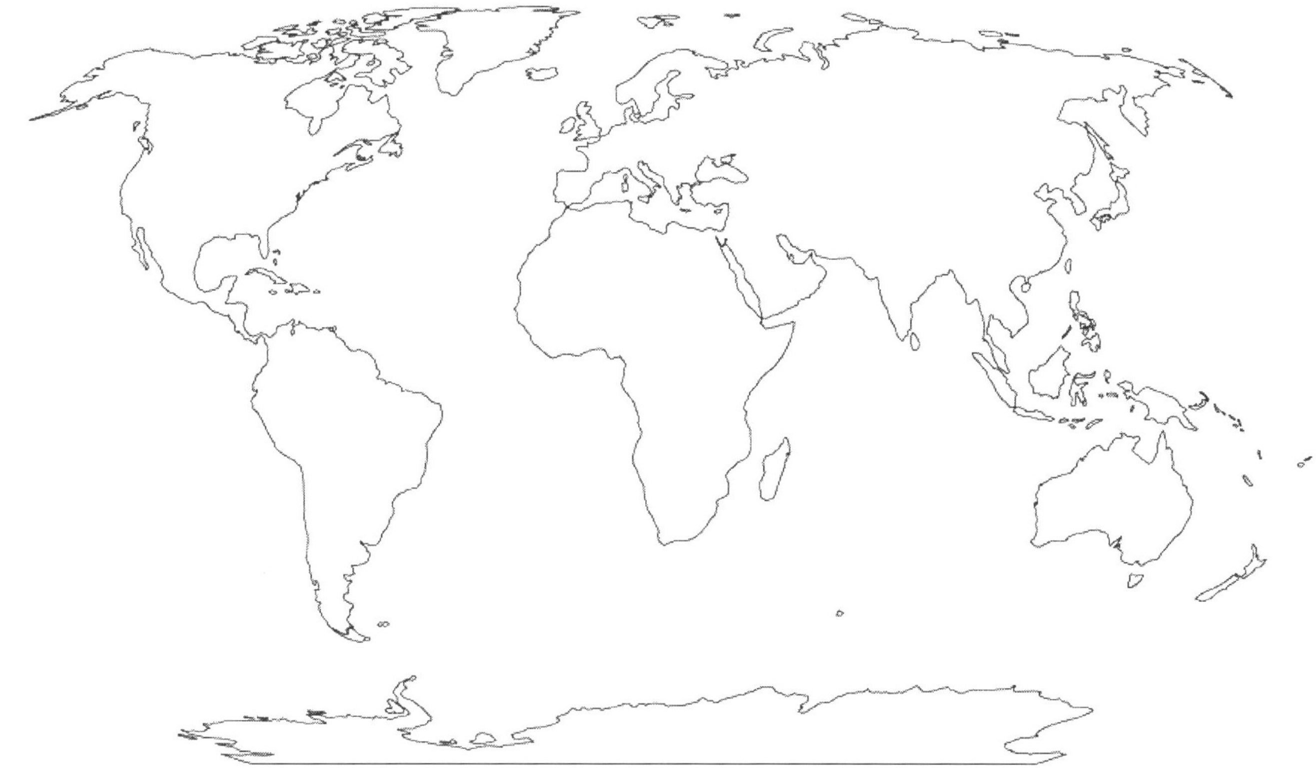

SEAS

Do some research, answer the questions, and write down three facts.

What is a sea?

Interesting fact about seas:

How many seas are there in the world?

What is the largest sea in the world?

Fascinating fact about seas:

Draw some creatures, plants, and trees that could be found in or around a sea.

Do some research, and answer the questions.

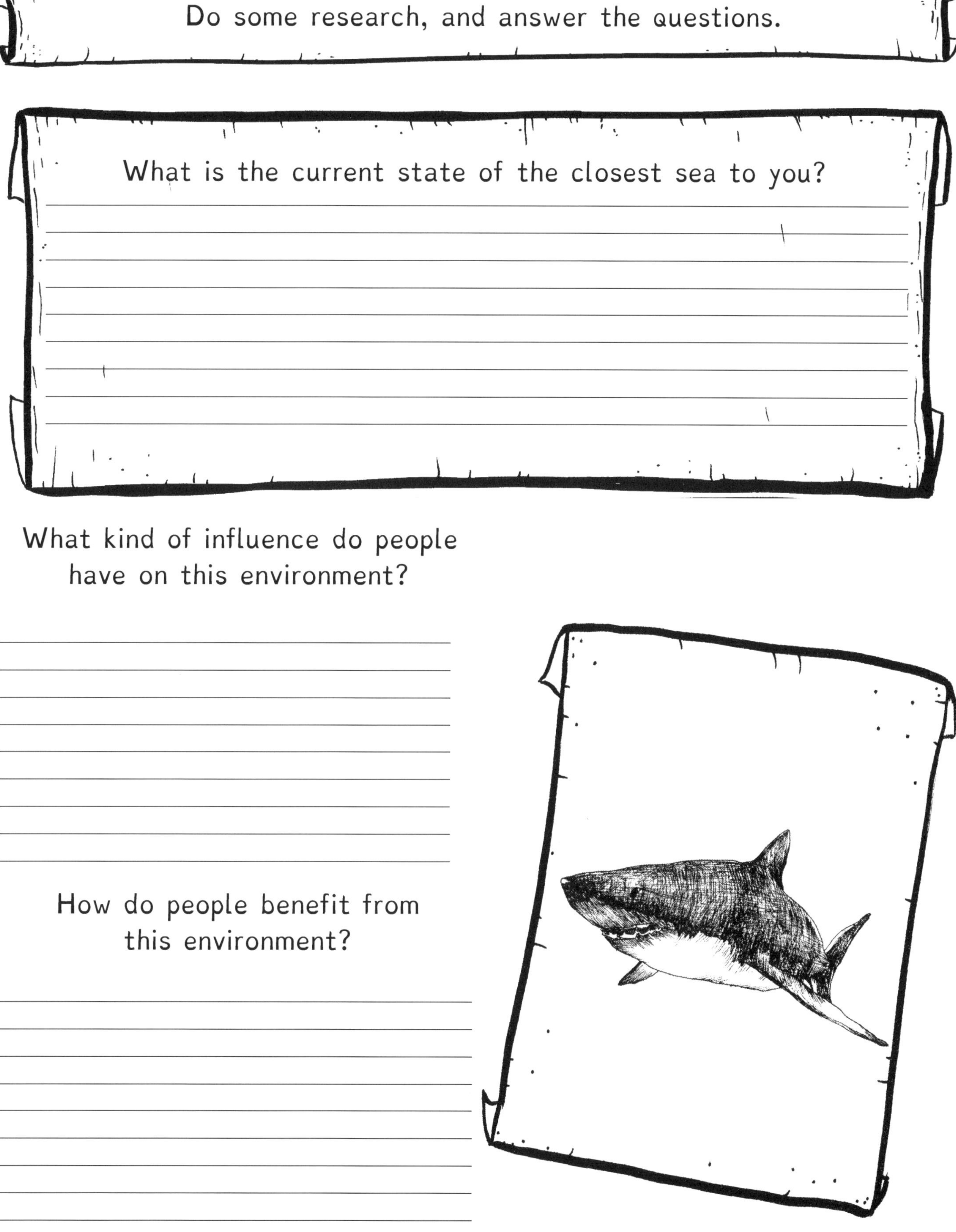

What is the current state of the closest sea to you?

What kind of influence do people have on this environment?

How do people benefit from this environment?

Do some research, and list the top five most well-known seas in the world. Write a short description for each one.

1. ______________________________

2. ______________________________

3. ______________________________

4. ______________________________

5. ______________________________

Mark on the map the location of the five seas.

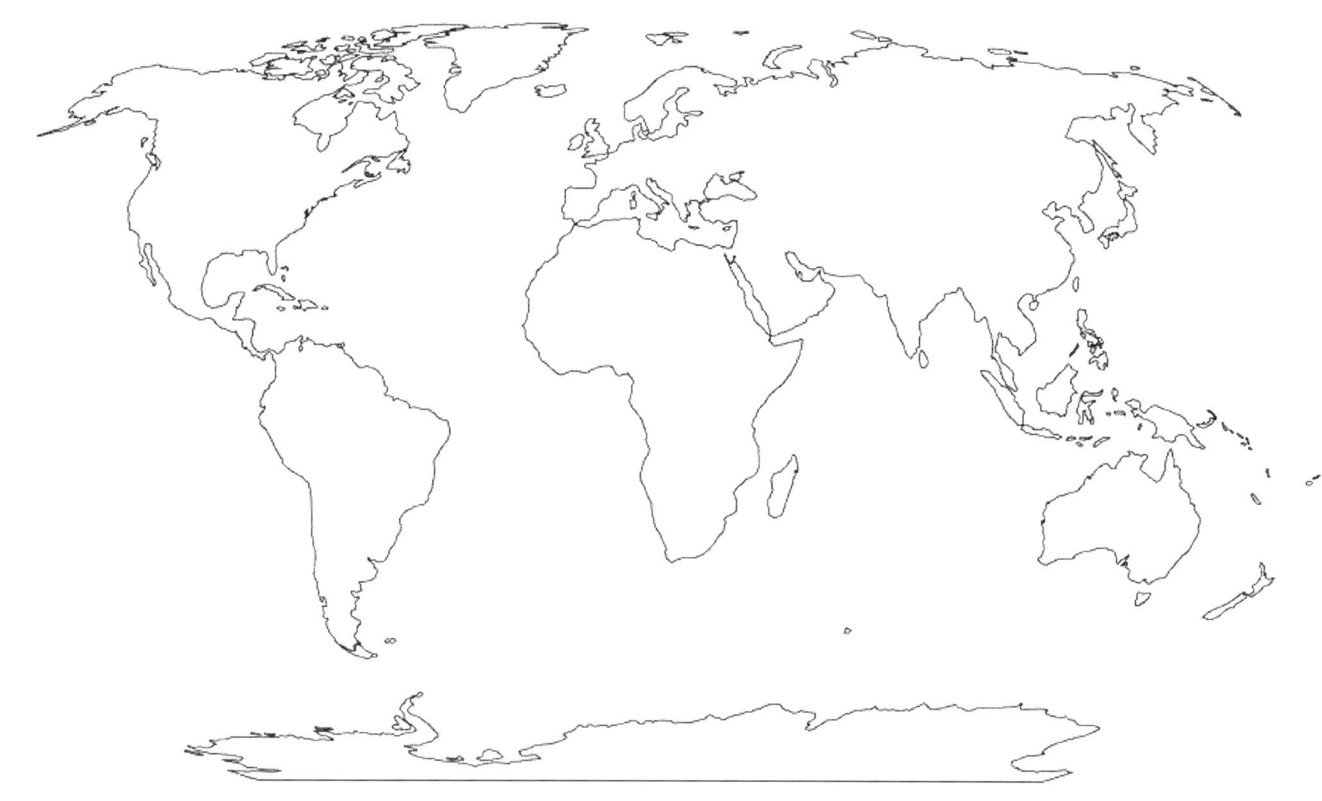

WATERFALLS

Do some research, answer the questions, and write down three facts.

What is a waterfall?

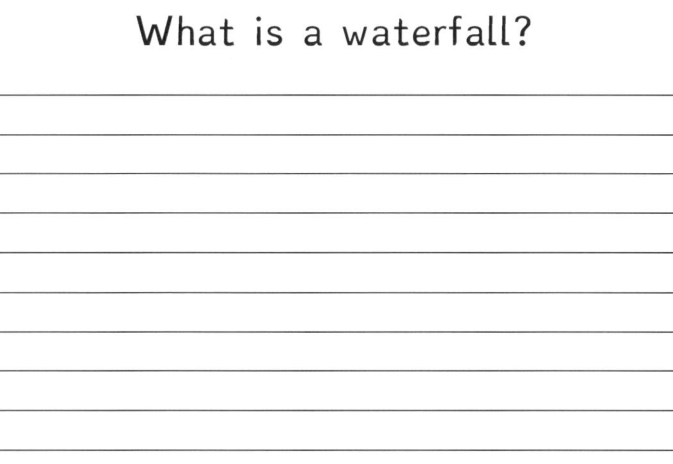

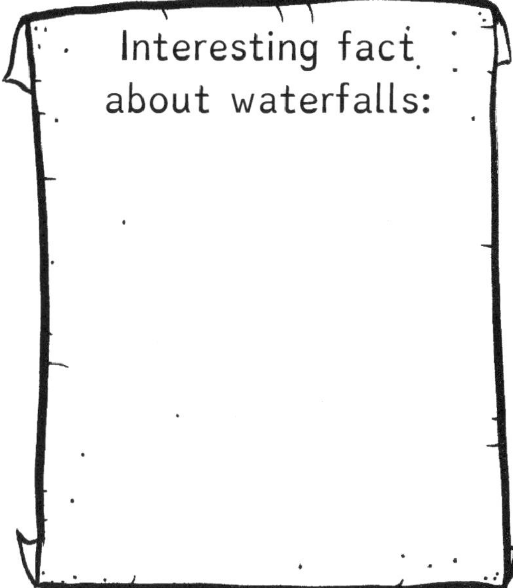

How do waterfalls form?

What is the largest waterfall in the world?

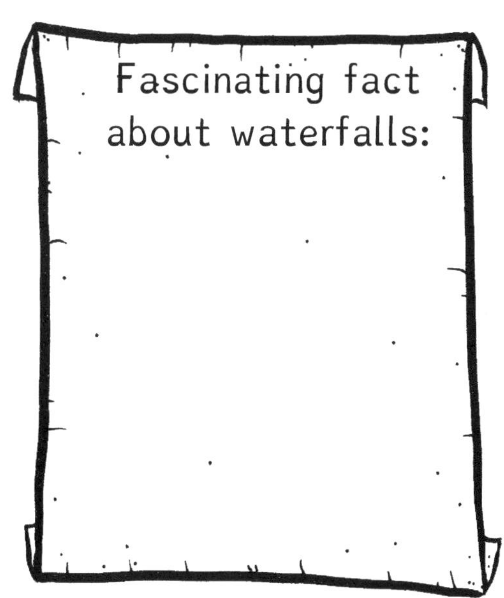

Draw some creatures, plants, and trees that could be found in or around a waterfall.

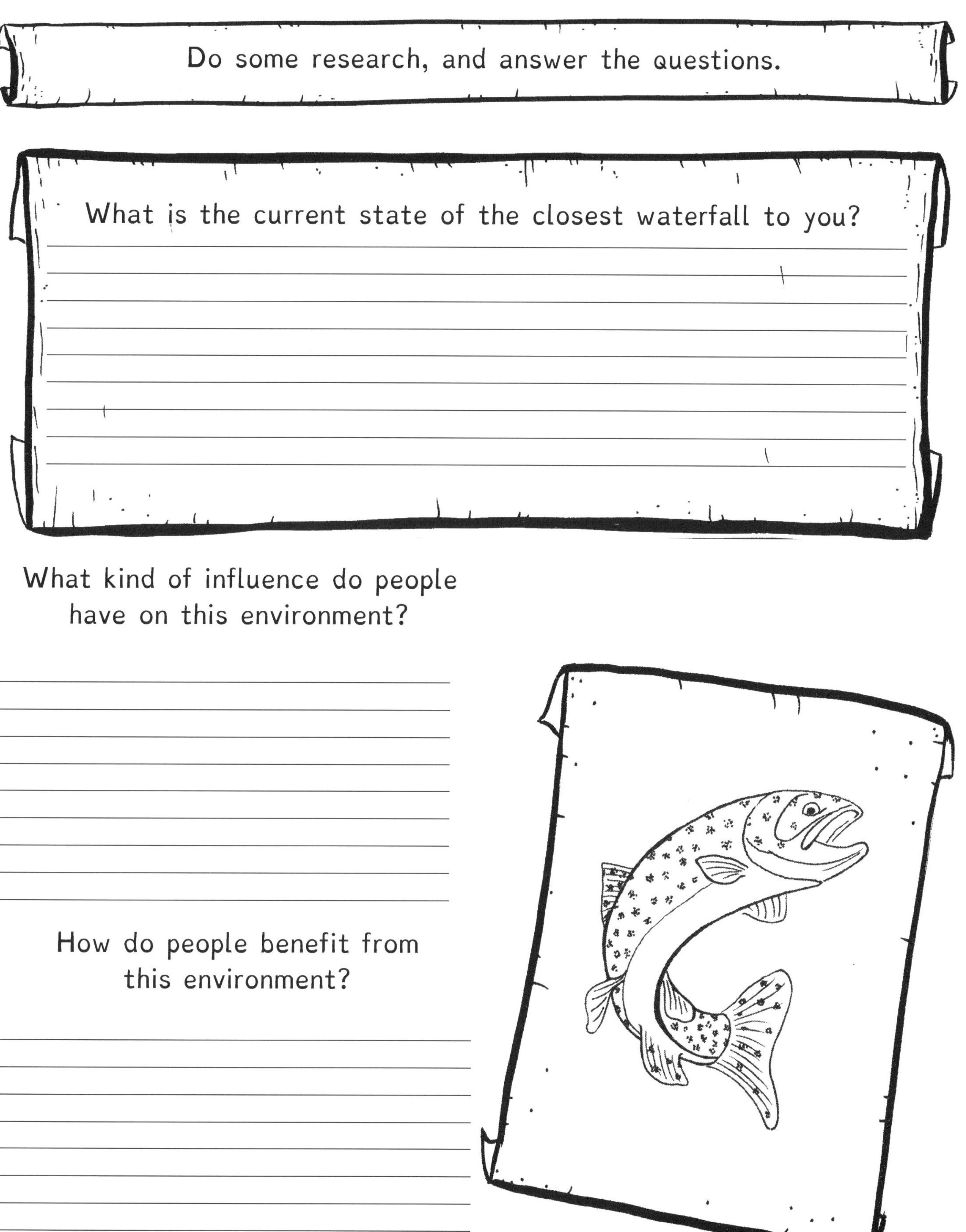
Do some research, and answer the questions.
What is the current state of the closest waterfall to you?
What kind of influence do people have on this environment?
How do people benefit from this environment?

Do some research, and list the top five most well-known waterfalls in the world. Write a short description for each one.

1.

2.

3.

4.

5.

Mark on the map the location of each waterfall.

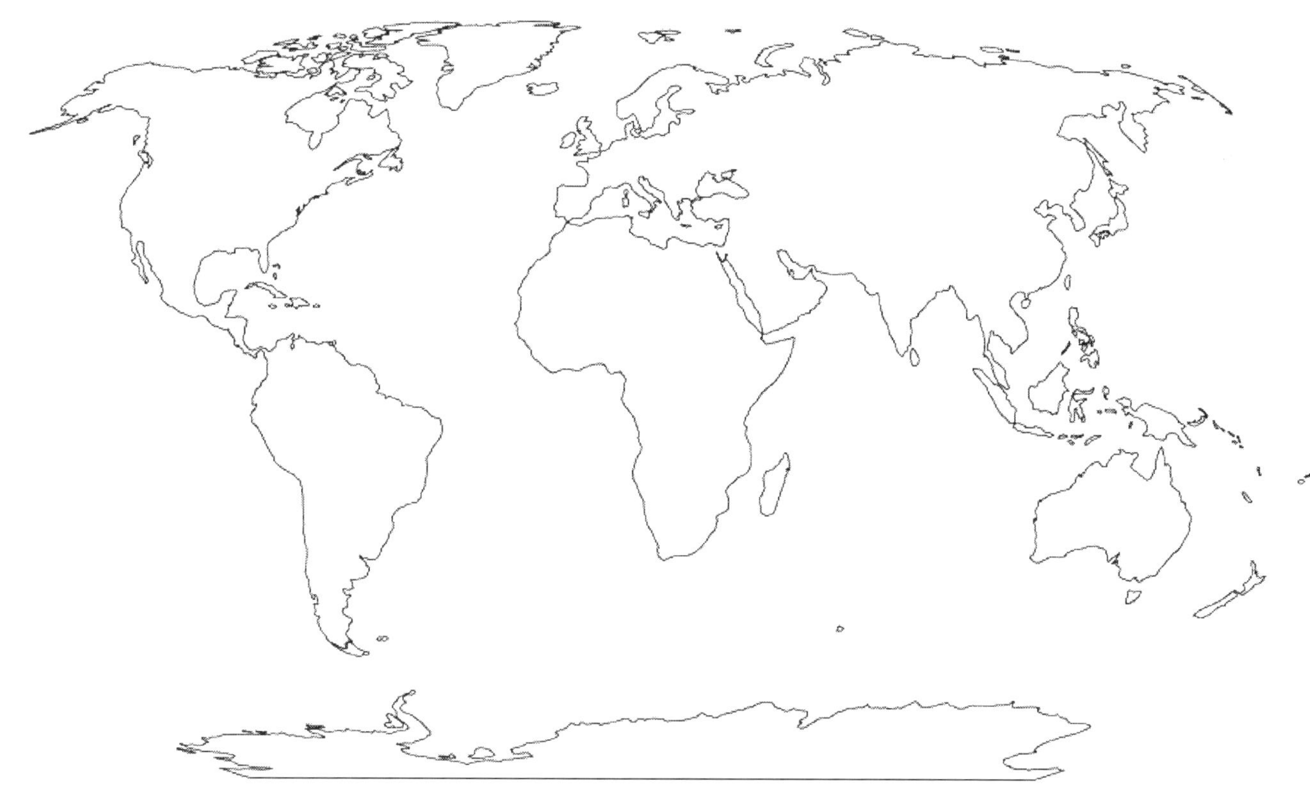

FORESTS

Do some research, answer the questions, and write down three facts.

What is a forest?

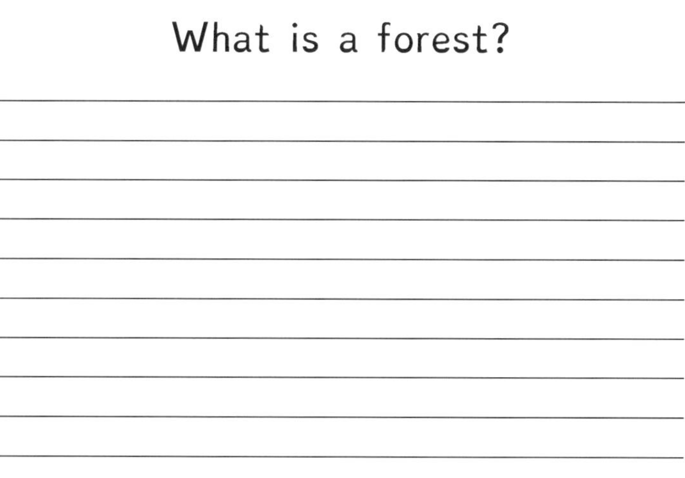

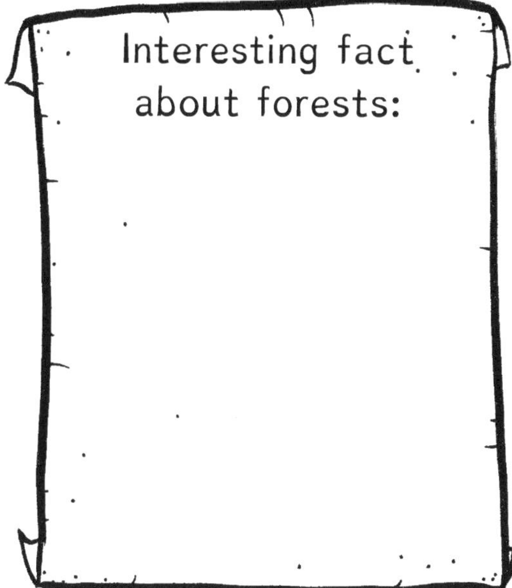

Interesting fact about forests:

Fun fact about forests:

What types of forests are there?

What is the largest forest in the world?

Fascinating fact about forests:

Draw some creatures, plants, and trees that could be found in a forest.

Do some research, and answer the questions.

What is the current state of the closest forest to you?

What kind of influence do people have on this environment?

How do people benefit from this environment?

Do some research, and list the top five most well-known forests in the world. Write a short description for each one.

1. ______________________________

2. ______________________________

3. ______________________________

4. ______________________________

5. ______________________________

Mark on the map the location of each forest.

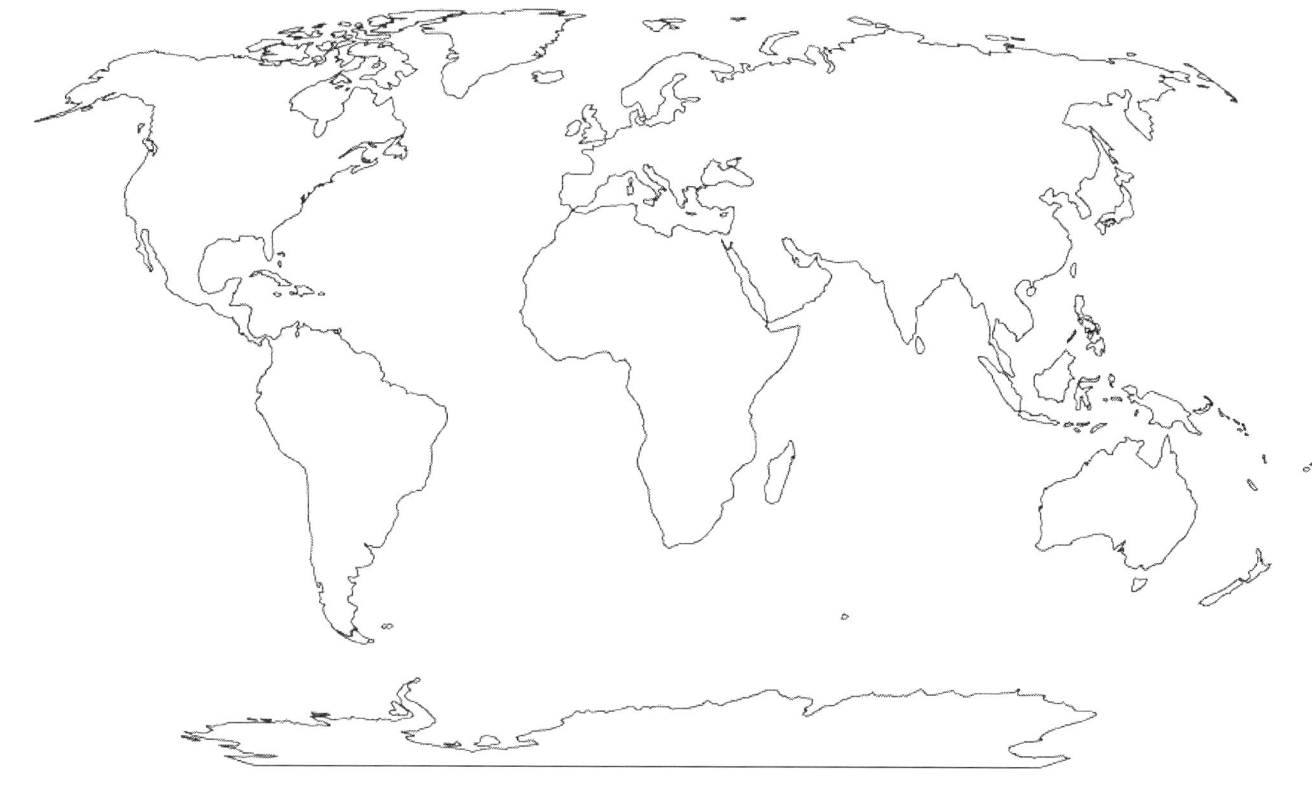

LAGOONS

Do some research, answer the questions, and write down three facts.

What is a lagoon?

Interesting fact about lagoons:

Fun fact about lagoons:

What are the different types of lagoons?

How are lagoons formed?

Fascinating fact about lagoons:

Draw some creatures, plants, and trees that could be found in or around a lagoon.

Do some research, and answer the questions.
What is the current state of the closest lagoon to you?
What kind of influence do people have on this environment?
How do people benefit from this environment?

Do some research, and list the top five most well-known lagoons in the world. Write a short description for each one.

1. ______________________________

2. ______________________________

3. ______________________________

4. ______________________________

5. ______________________________

Mark on the map the location of each lagoon.

DESERTS

Do some research, answer the questions, and write down three facts.

What is a desert?

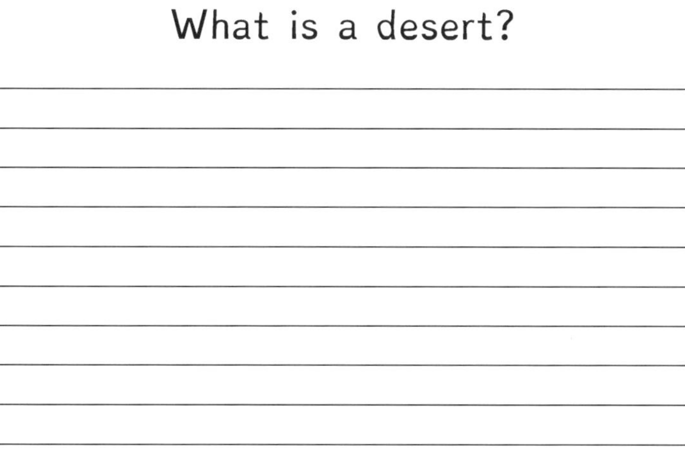

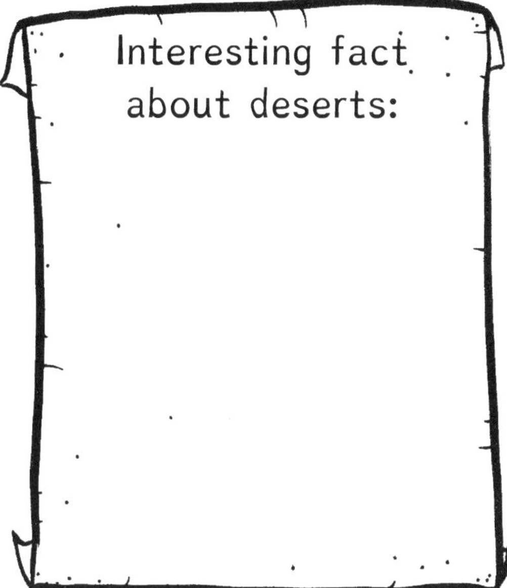

What are the different types of deserts?

What is the largest desert in the world?

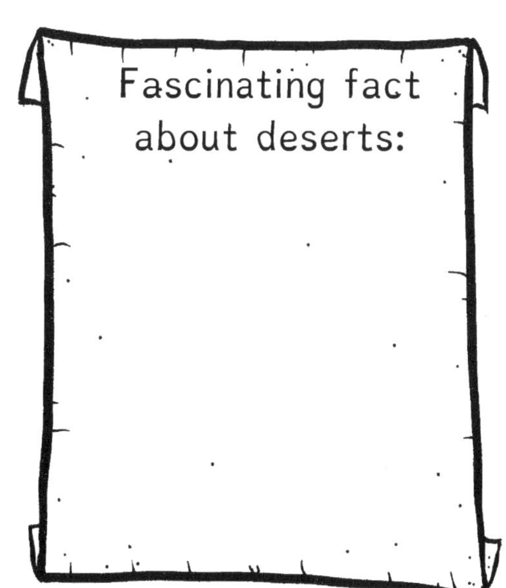

Draw some creatures, plants, and trees
that could be found in a desert.

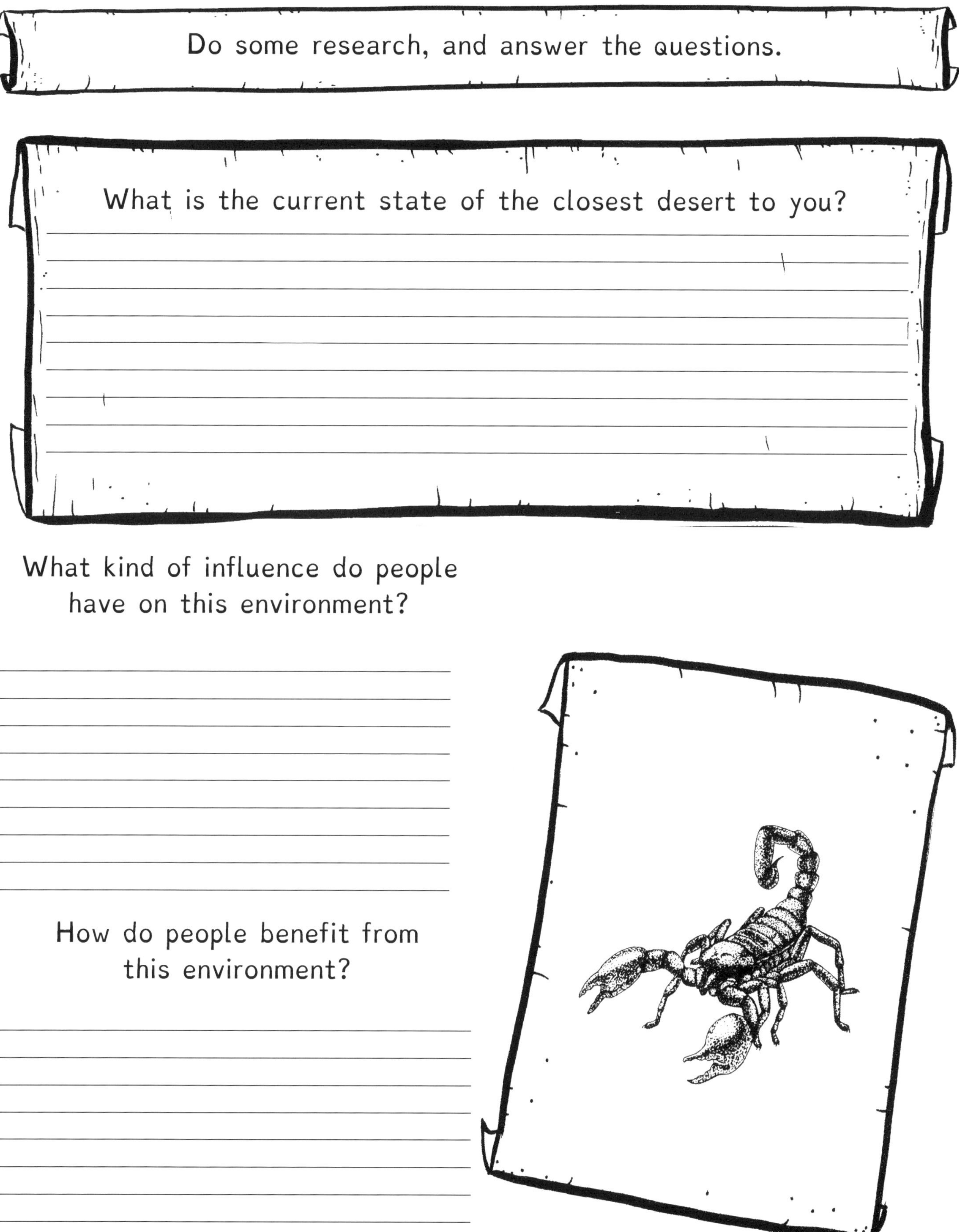

Do some research, and answer the questions.

What is the current state of the closest desert to you?

What kind of influence do people have on this environment?

How do people benefit from this environment?

Do some research, and list the top five most well-known deserts in the world. Write a short description for each one.

1.

2.

3.

4.

5.

Mark on the map the location of each desert.

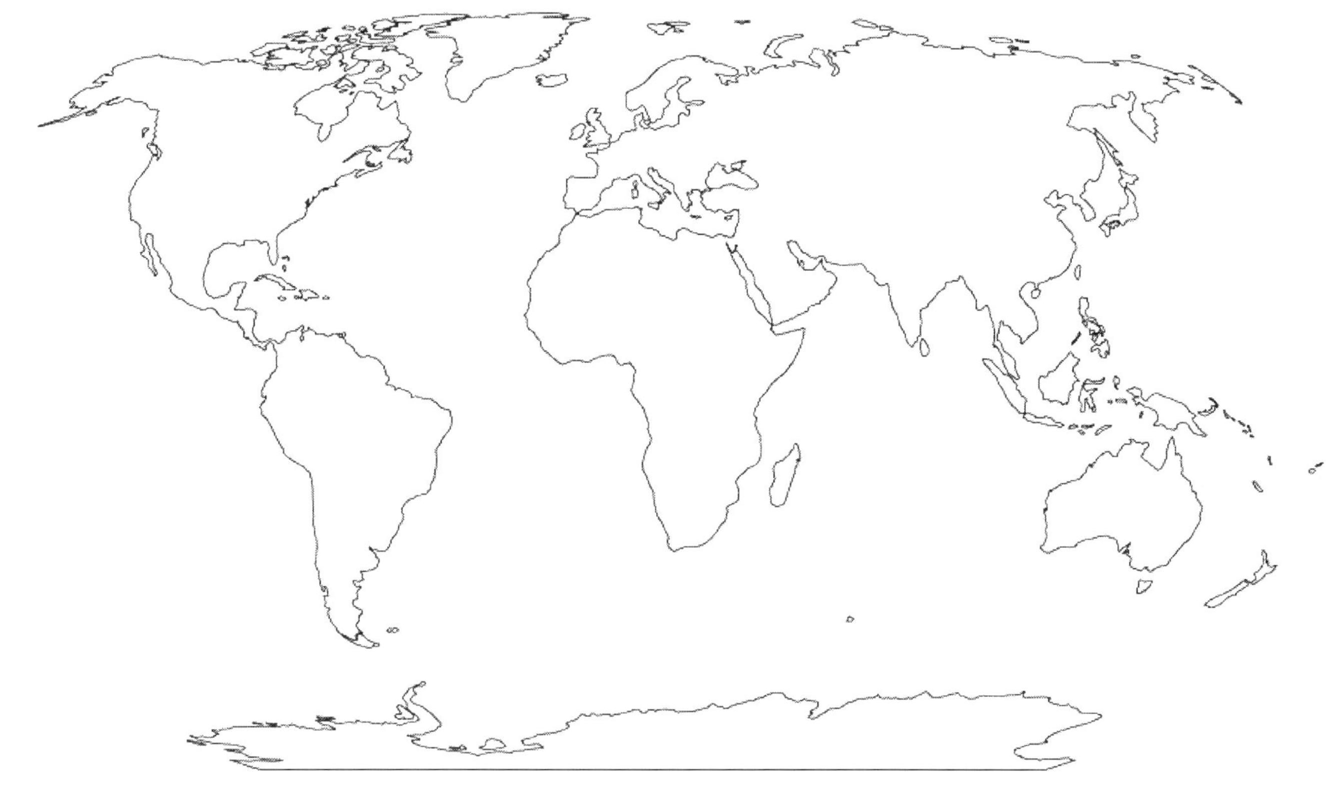

GLACIERS

Do some research, answer the questions, and write down some facts.

What is a glacier?

Interesting fact about glaciers:

What are the different types of glaciers?

How do glaciers form?

Fascinating fact about glaciers:

Draw some creatures that could be found on or around a glacier.

Do some research, and answer the questions.

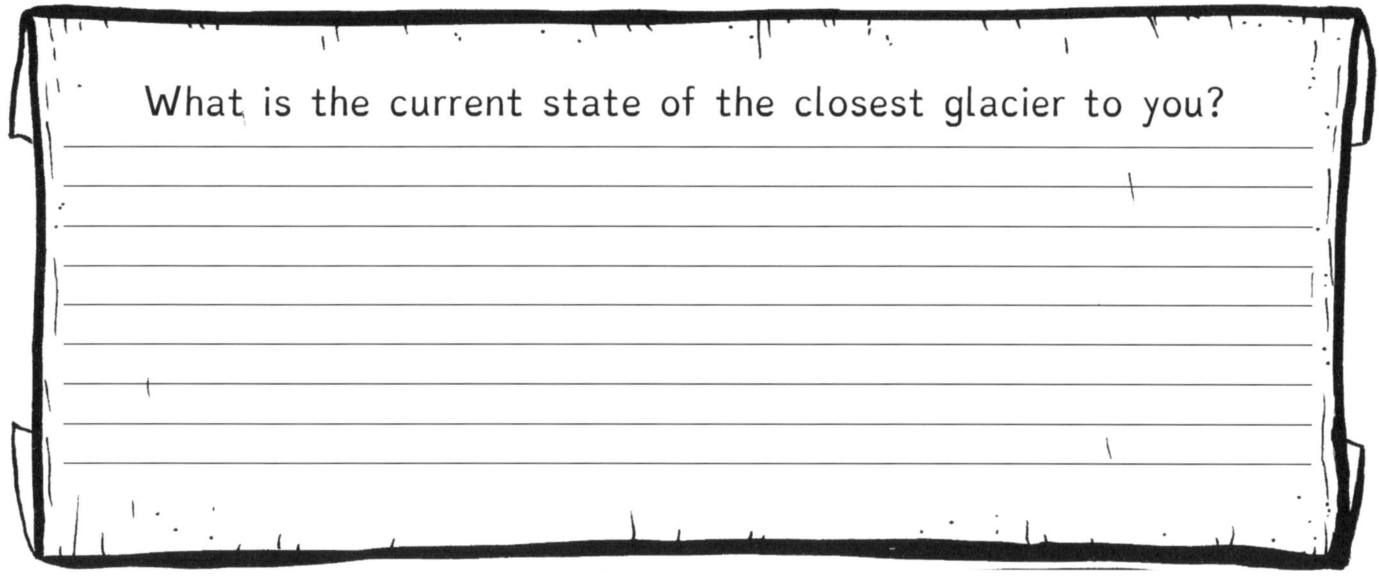

What is the current state of the closest glacier to you?

What kind of influence do people have on this environment?

How do people benefit from this environment?

Do some research, and list the top five most well-known glaciers in the world. Write a short description for each one.

1.

2.

3.

4.

5.

Mark on the map the location of each glacier.

PONDS

Do some research, answer the questions, and write down three facts.

What is a pond?

Interesting fact about ponds:

Fun fact about ponds:

What is the difference between ponds and lakes?

How are ponds formed?

Fascinating fact about ponds:

Draw some creatures, plants, and trees that could be found in or around a pond.

Do some research, and answer the questions.

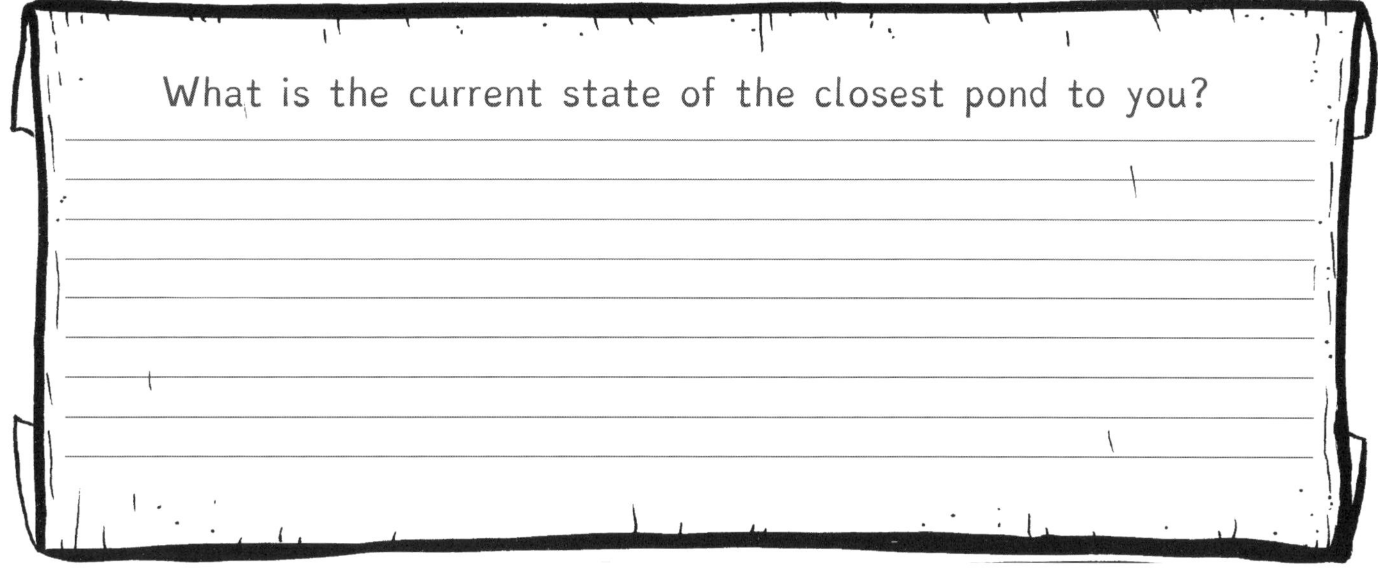

What is the current state of the closest pond to you?

What kind of influence do people have on this environment?

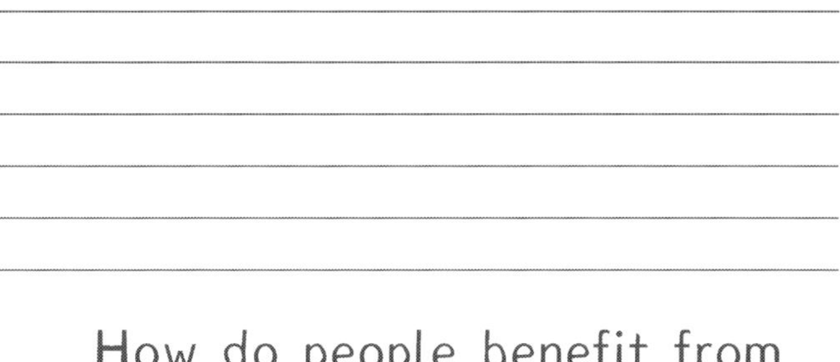

How do people benefit from this environment?

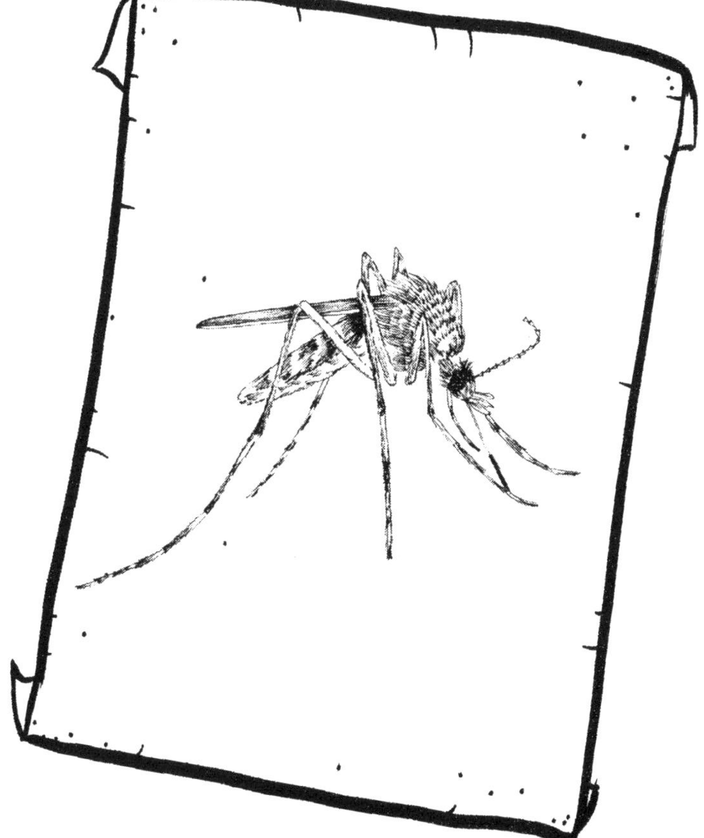

STREAMS

Do some research, answer the questions, and write down three facts.

What is a stream?

Interesting fact about streams:

Fun fact about streams:

What are the different types of streams?

How do streams form?

Fascinating fact about streams:

Draw some creatures, plants, and trees that could be found in or around a stream.

Do some research, and answer the questions.

What is the current state of the closest stream to you?

What kind of influence do people have on this environment?

How do people benefit from this environment?

CANYONS

Do some research, answer the questions, and write down three facts.

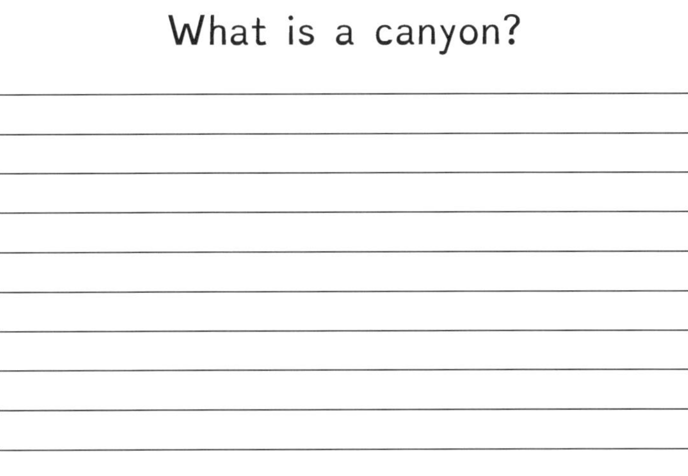

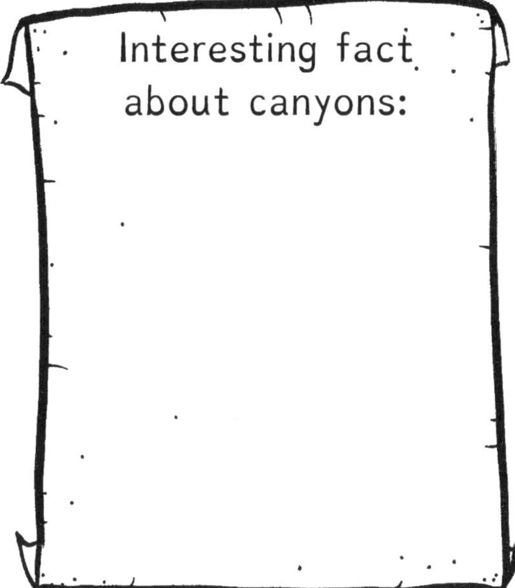

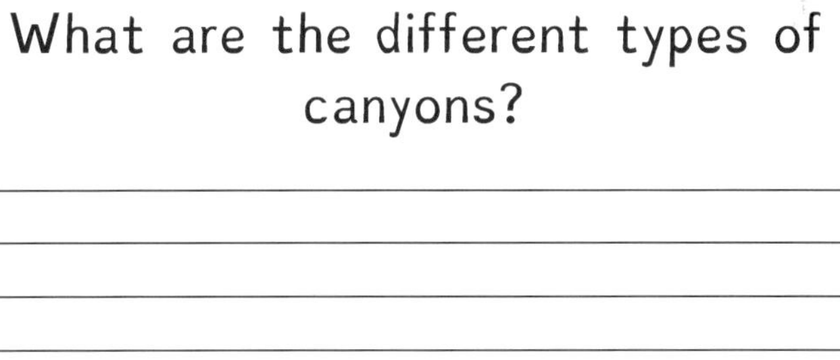

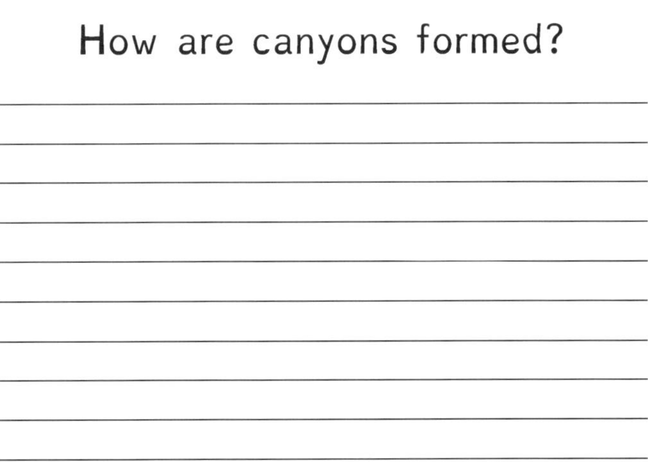

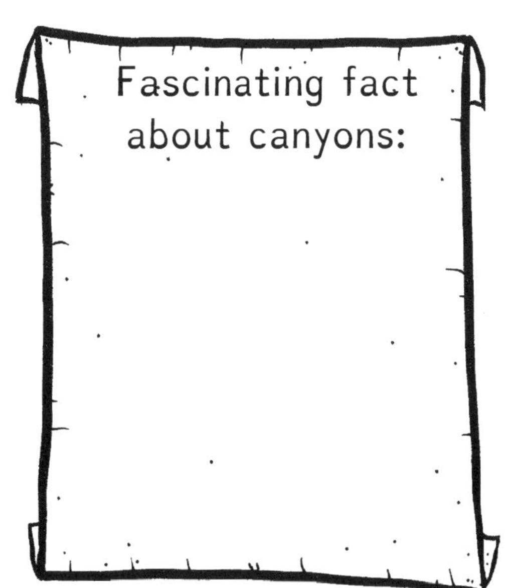

Draw some creatures, plants, and trees that could be found in or around a canyon.

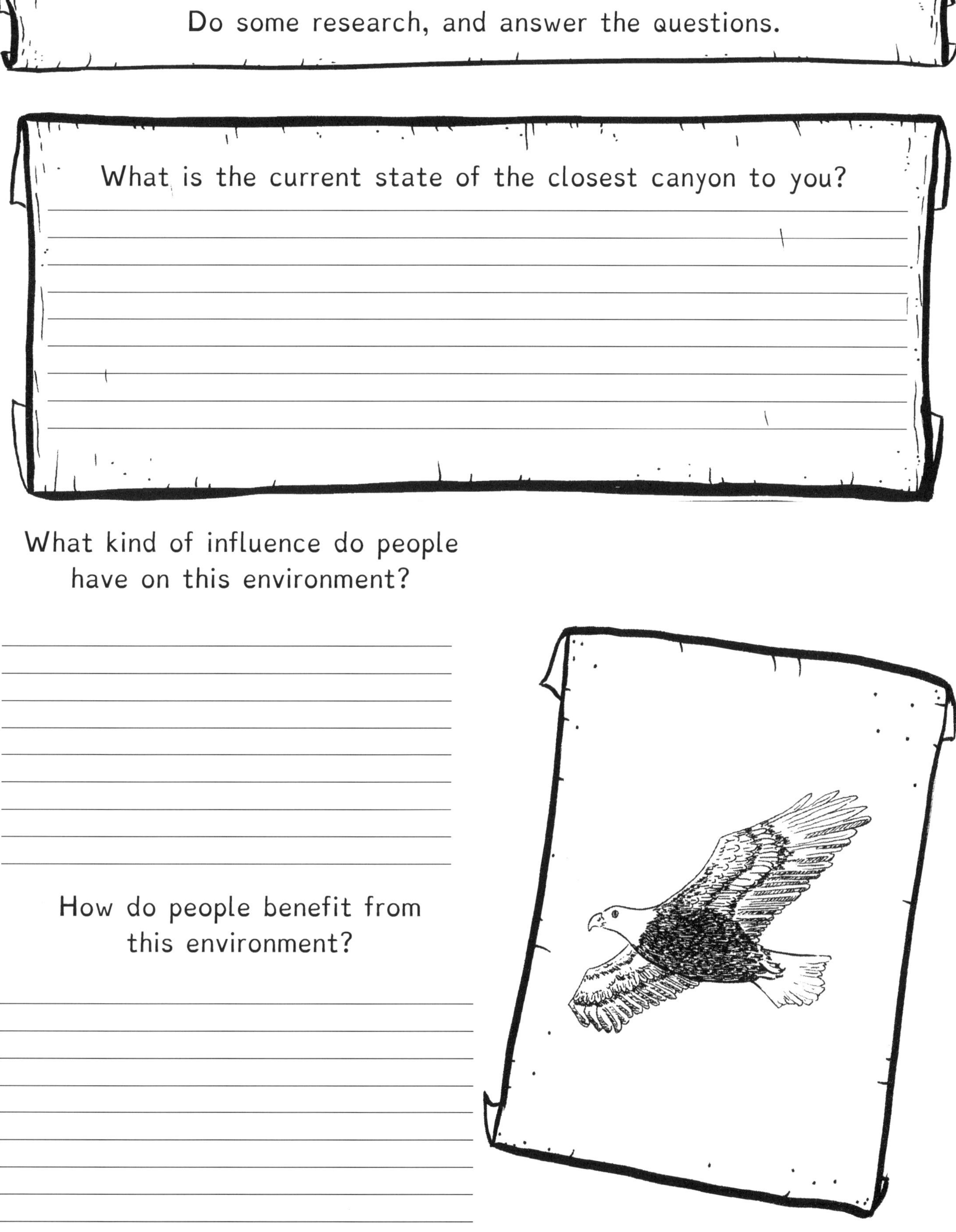

Do some research, and answer the questions.

What is the current state of the closest canyon to you?

What kind of influence do people have on this environment?

How do people benefit from this environment?

Do some research, and list the top five most well-known canyons in the world. Write a short description for each one.

1. ______________________________

2. ______________________________

3. ______________________________

4. ______________________________

5. ______________________________

Mark on the map the location of each canyon.

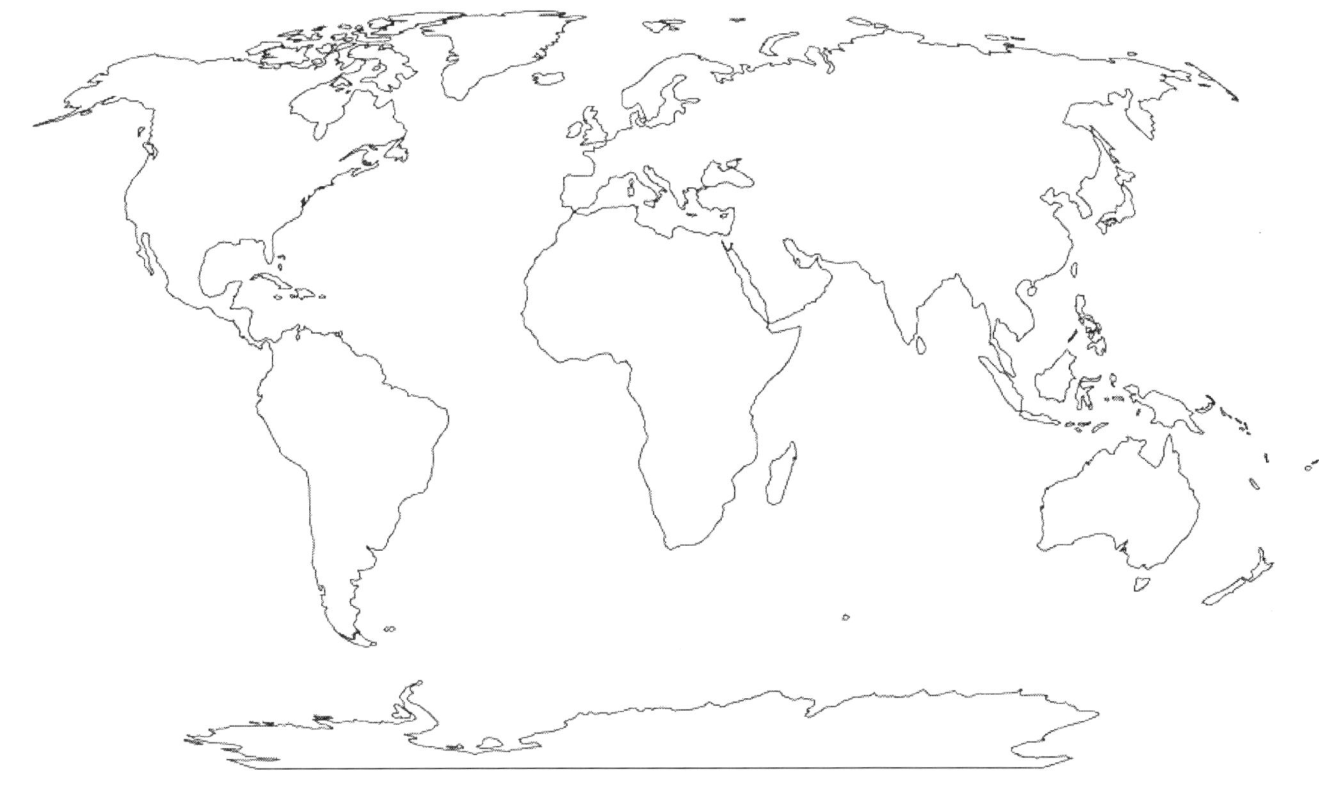

ISLANDS

Do some research, answer the questions, and write down three facts.

What is an island?

Interesting fact about islands:

Fun fact about islands:

What are the different types of islands?

How do islands form?

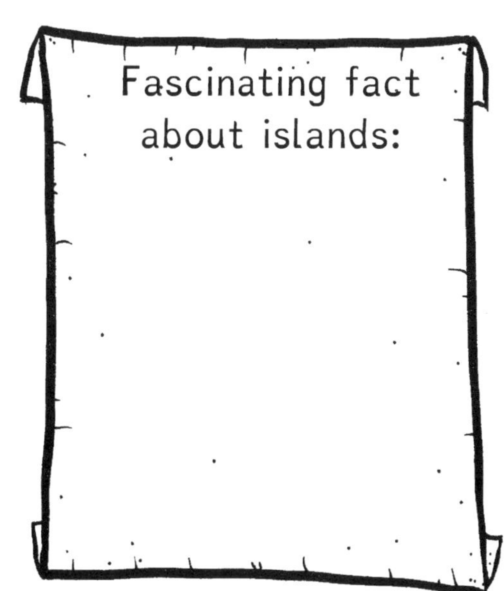

Fascinating fact about islands:

Draw some creatures, plants, and trees that could be found on an island.

Do some research, and answer the questions.

What is the current state of the closest island to you?

What kind of influence do people have on this environment?

How do people benefit from this environment?

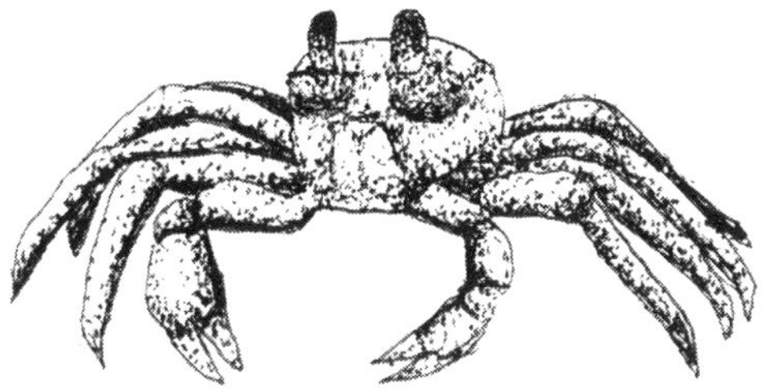

Do some research, and list the top five most well-known islands in the world. Write a short description for each one.

1. ____________________

2. ____________________

3. ____________________

4. ____________________

5. ____________________

Mark on the map the location of each island.

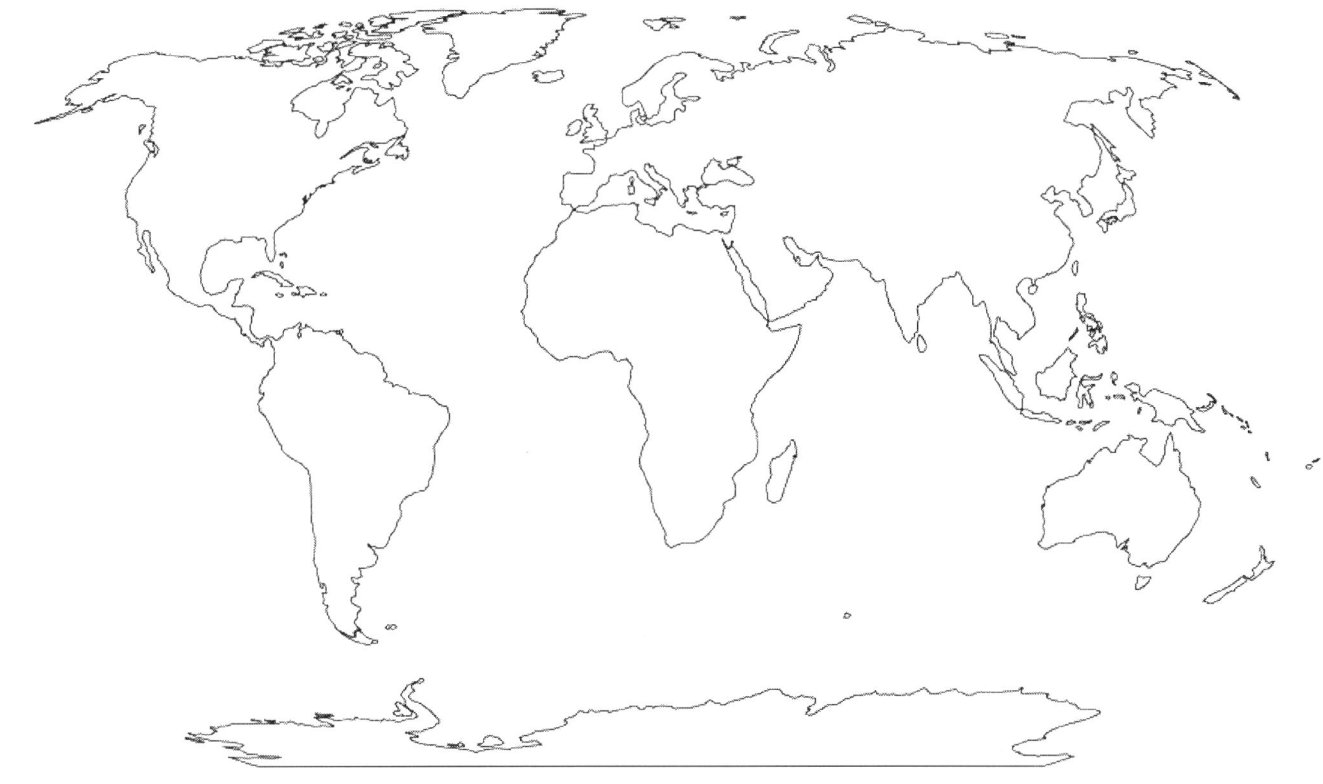

PLATEAUS

Do some research, answer the questions, and write down three facts.

What is a plateau?

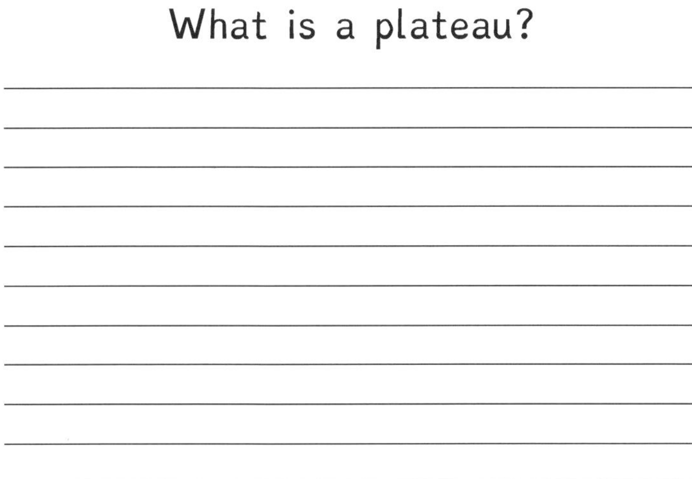

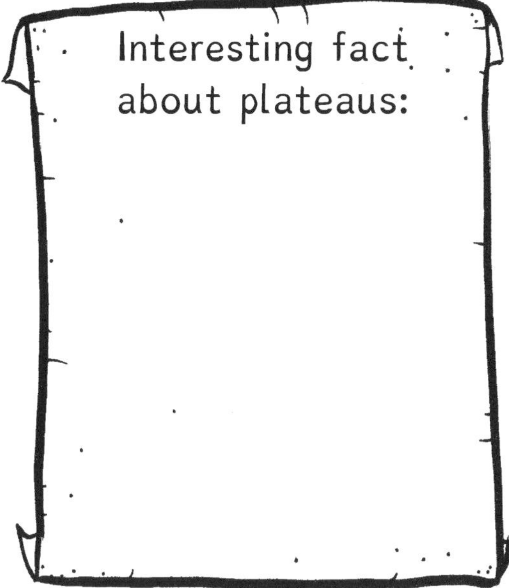

How are plateaus formed?

What is the largest plateau in the world?

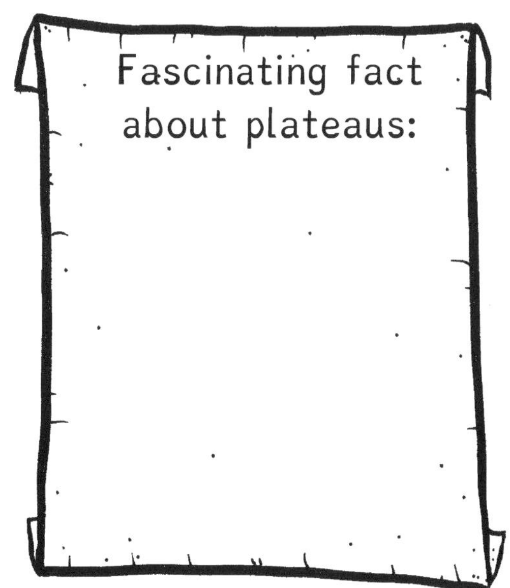

Draw some creatures, plants, and trees that could be found on a plateau.

Do some research, and answer the questions.

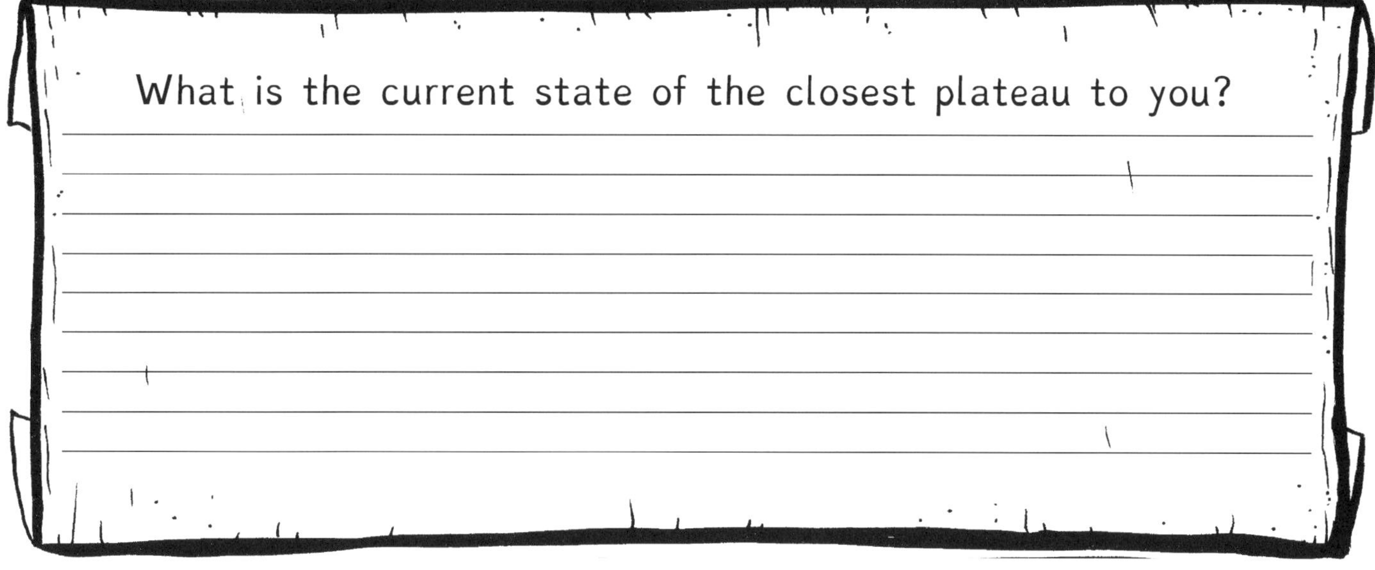

What is the current state of the closest plateau to you?

What kind of influence do people have on this environment?

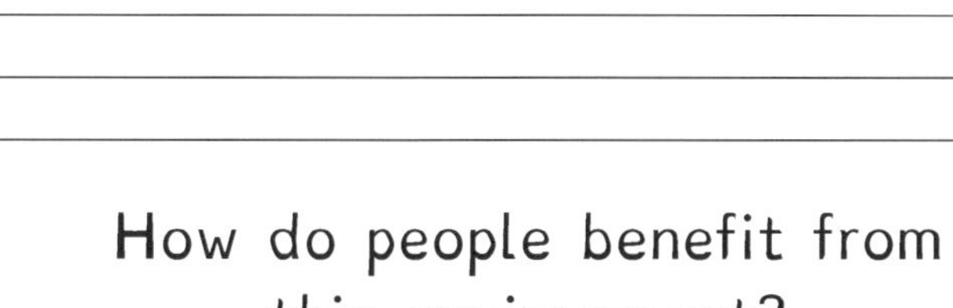

How do people benefit from this environment?

Do some research, and list the top five most well-known plateaus in the world. Write a short description for each one.

1. ______________________________

2. ______________________________

3. ______________________________

4. ______________________________

5. ______________________________

Mark on the map the location of each plateau.

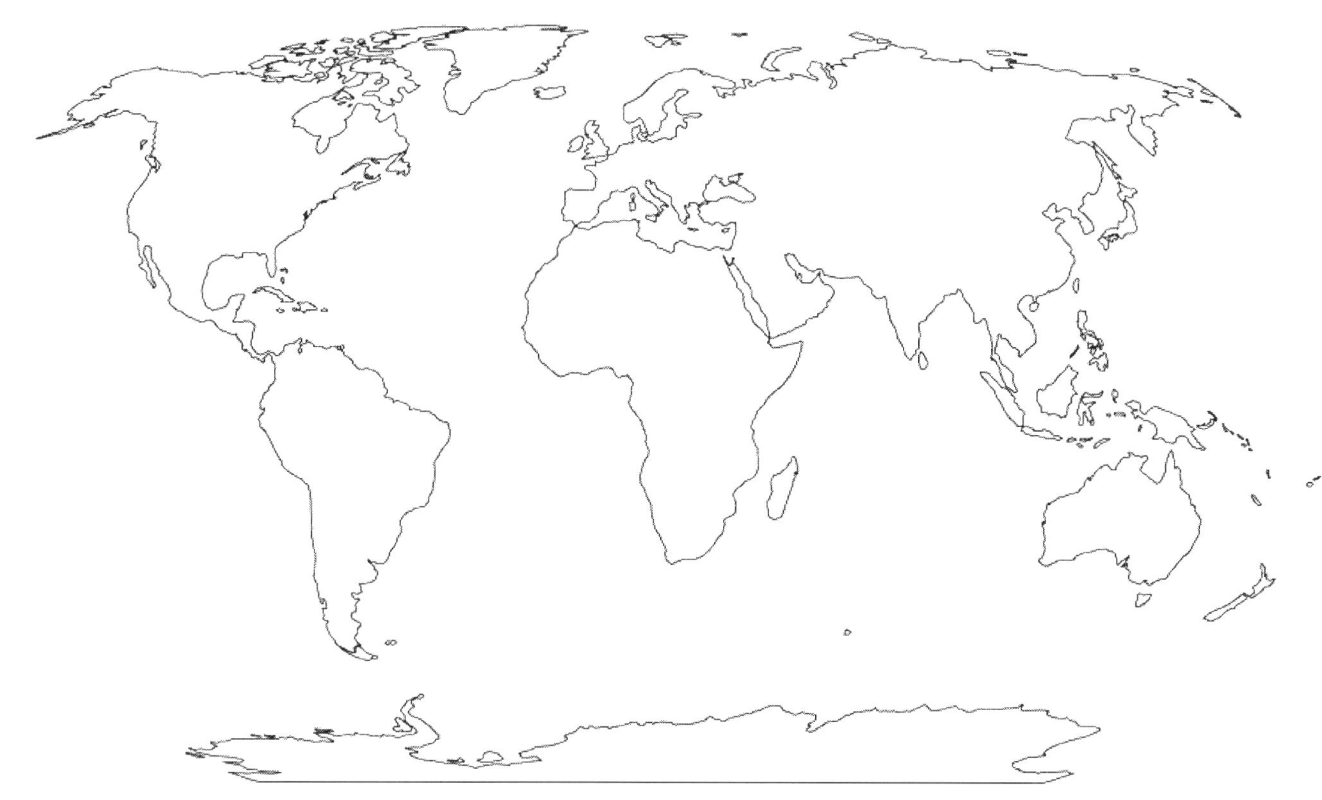

HOT SPRINGS

Do some research, answer the questions, and write down some facts.

What is a hot spring?

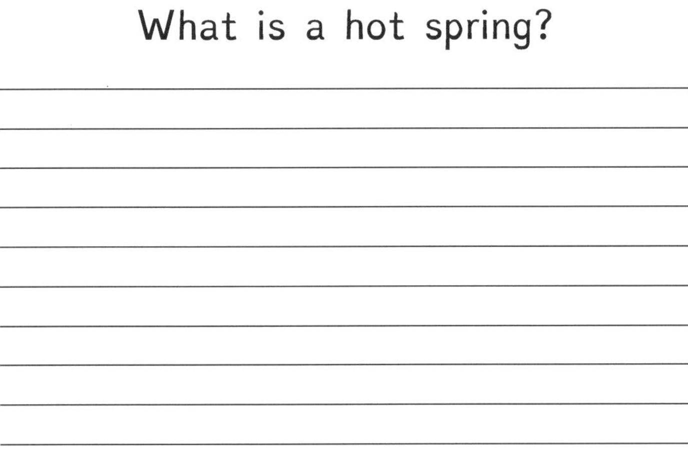

Interesting fact about hot springs:

Fun fact about hot springs:

What are the different types of hot springs?

What makes the water in hot springs hot?

Fascinating fact about hot springs:

Draw some creatures, plants, and trees that could be found in or around a hot spring.

Do some research, and answer the questions.

What is the current state of the closest hot spring to you?

What kind of influence do people have on this environment?

How do people benefit from this environment?

Do some research, and list the top five most well-known hot springs in the world. Write a short description for each one.

1. ______________________________

2. ______________________________

3. ______________________________

4. ______________________________

5. ______________________________

Mark on the map the location of each hot spring.

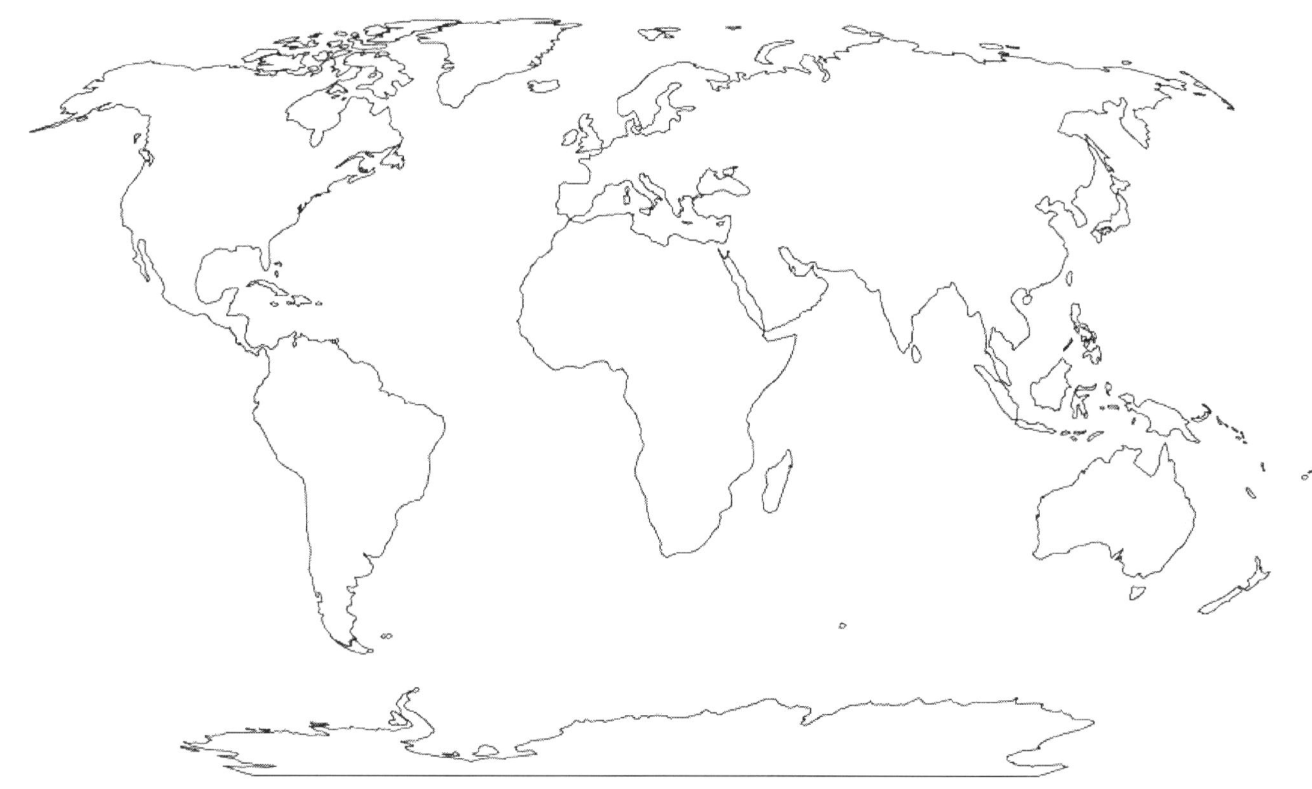

PLAINS

Do some research, answer the questions, and write down three facts.

What is a plain?

Interesting fact about plains:

Fun fact about plains:

What are the different types of plains?

How are plains formed?

Fascinating fact about plains:

Draw some creatures, plants, and trees that could be found in a plain.

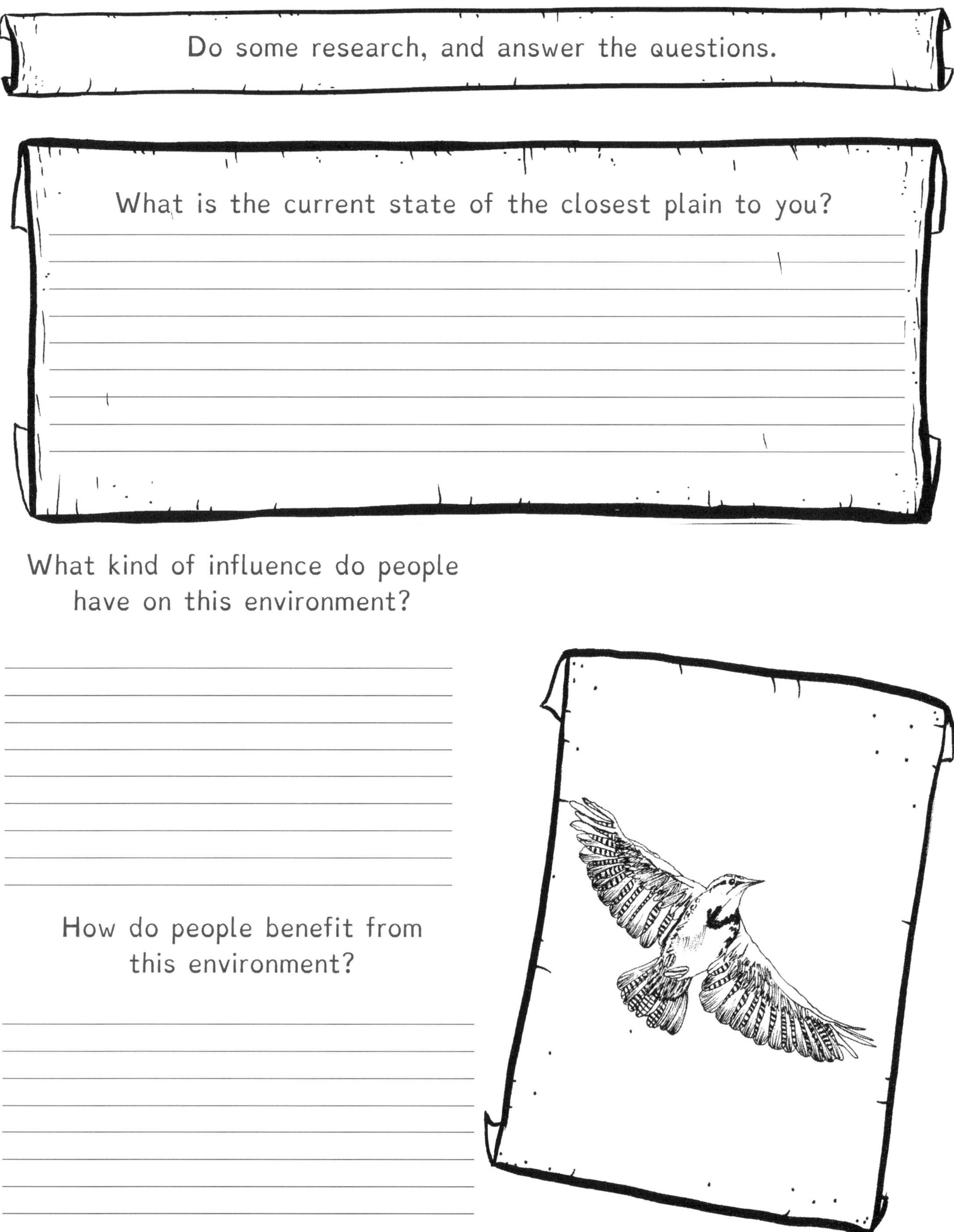

Do some research, and answer the questions.
What is the current state of the closest plain to you?
What kind of influence do people have on this environment?
How do people benefit from this environment?

Do some research, and list the top five most well-known plains in the world. Write a short description for each one.

1.

2.

3.

4.

5.

Mark on the map the location of each plain.

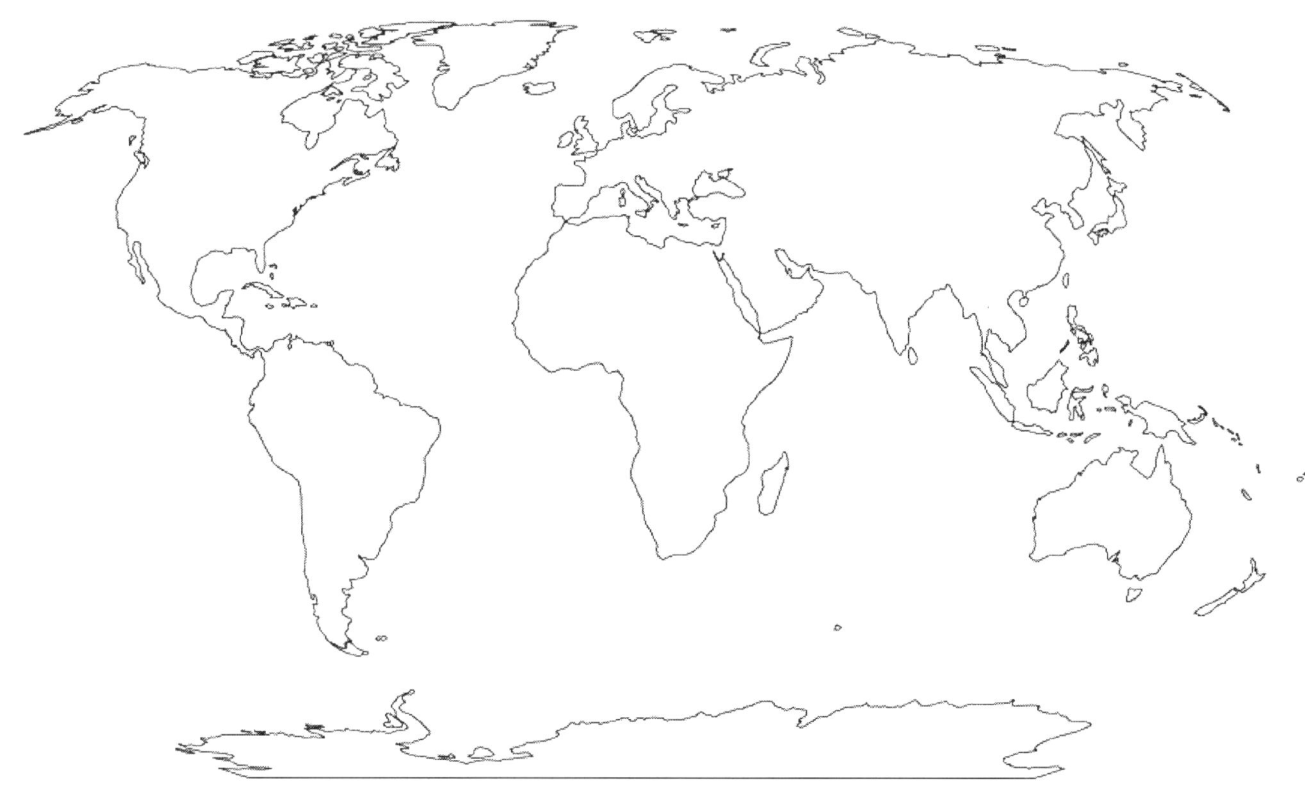

OASES

Do some research, answer the questions, and write down some facts.

What is an oasis?

Interesting fact about oases:

Fun fact about oases:

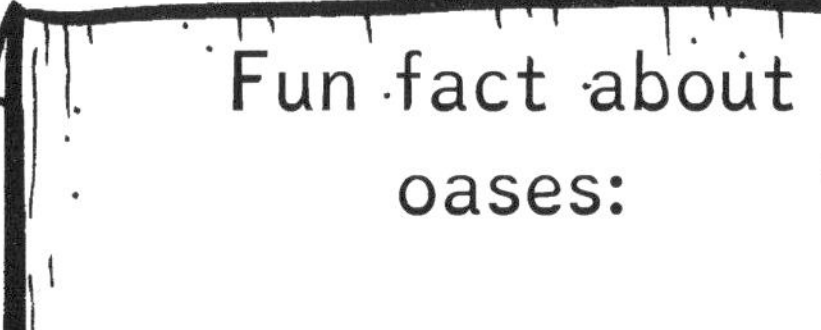

What is the largest oasis in the world?

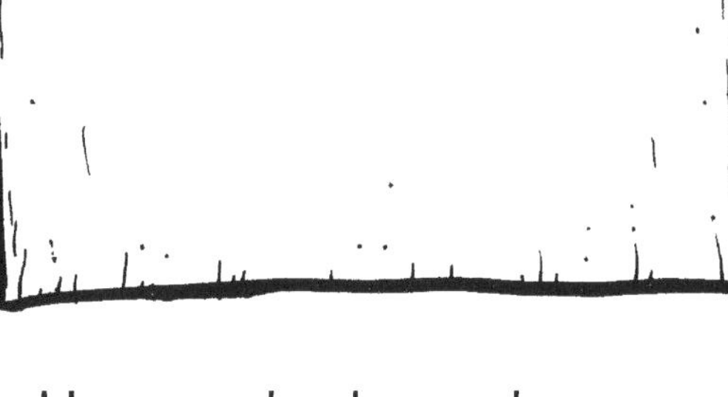

How and where does an oasis form?

Fascinating fact about oases:

Draw some creatures, plants, and trees that could be found in an oasis.

Do some research, and answer the questions.

What is the current state of the closest oasis to you?

What kind of influence do people have on this environment?

How do people benefit from this environment?

Do some research, and list the top five most well-known oases in the world. Write a short description for each one.

1. ______

2. ______

3. ______

4. ______

5. ______

Mark on the map the location of each oasis.

GEYSERS

Do some research, answer the questions, and write down three facts.

What is a geyser?

Interesting fact about geysers:

Fun fact about geysers:

Where can geysers occur?

How often do geysers erupt?

Do some research, and list the top five most well-known geysers in the world. Write a short description for each one.

1. ____________________

2. ____________________

3. ____________________

4. ____________________

5. ____________________

Mark on the map the location of each geyser.

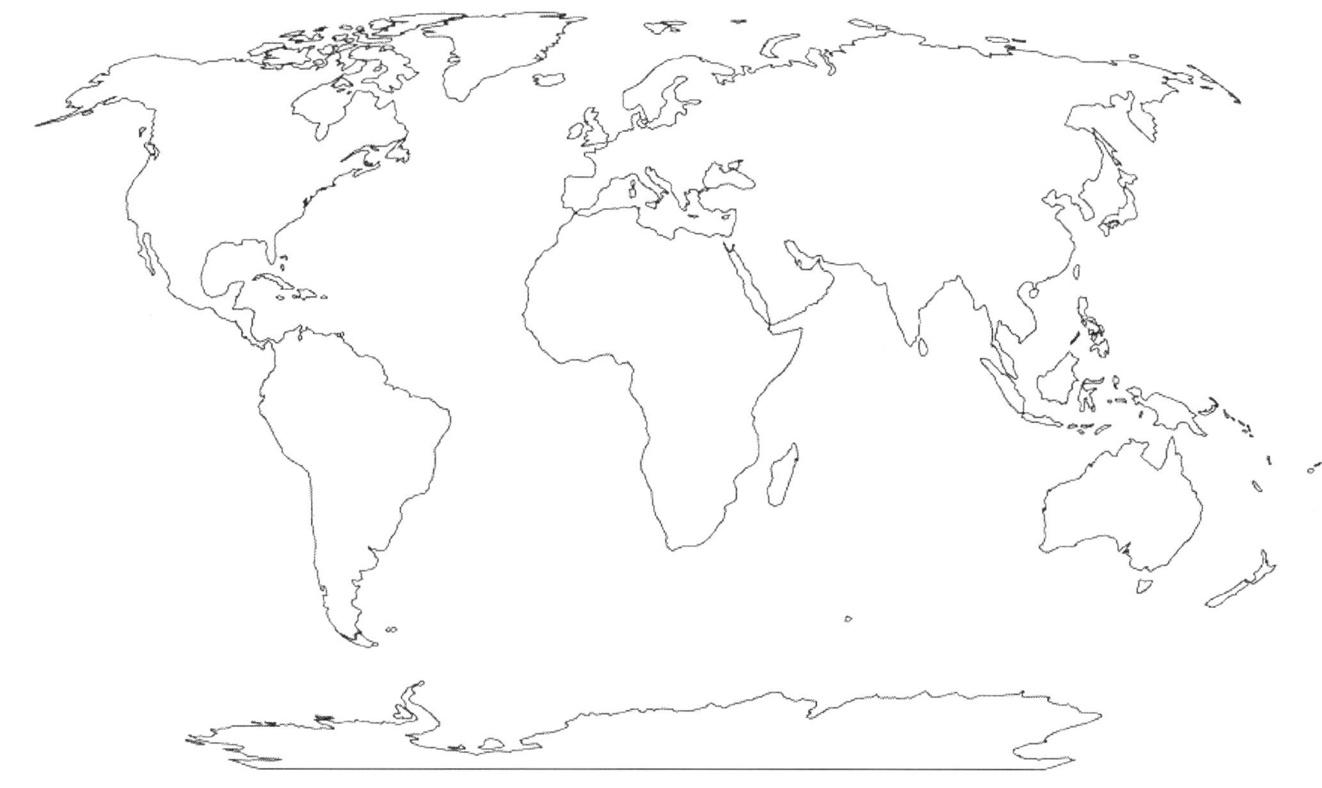

RAINFORESTS

Do some research, answer the questions, and write down three facts.

What is a rainforest?

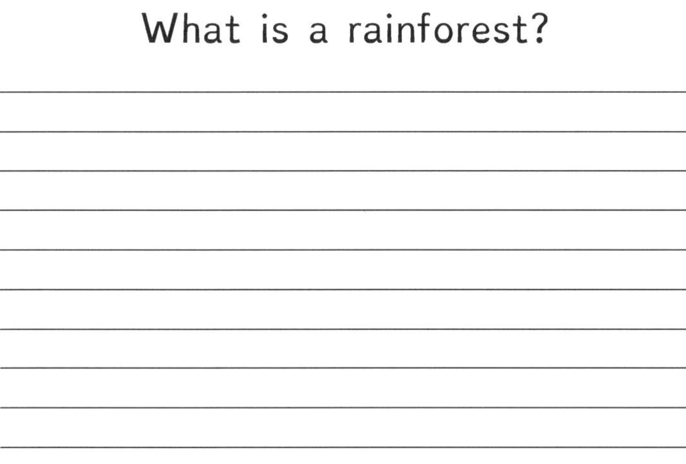

What are the different types of rainforests?

What is the largest rainforest in the world?

Draw some creatures, plants, and trees that could be found in a rainforest.

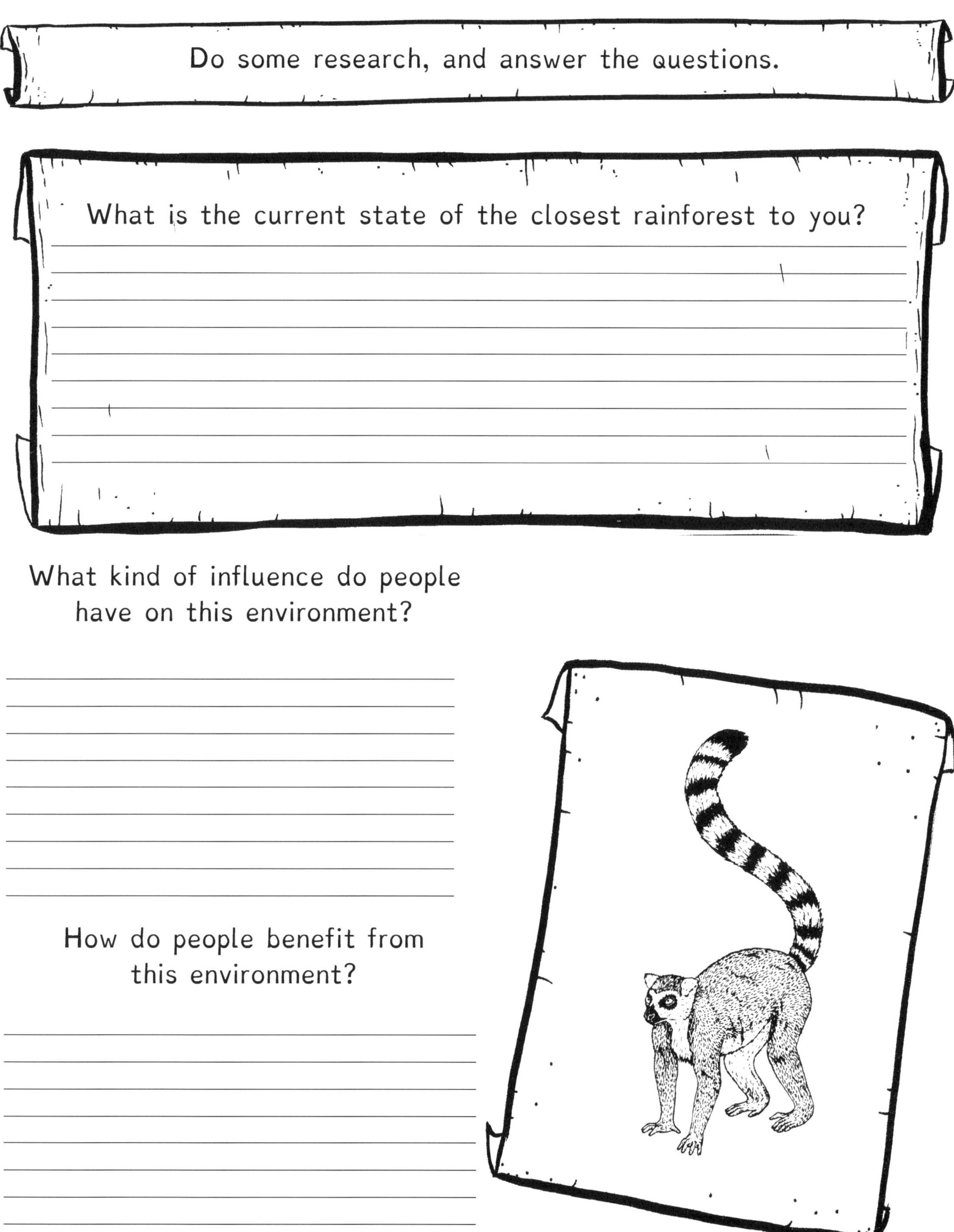

Do some research, and answer the questions.

What is the current state of the closest rainforest to you?

What kind of influence do people have on this environment?

How do people benefit from this environment?

Do some research, and list the top five most well-known rainforests in the world. Write a short description for each one.

1. ______________________________

2. ______________________________

3. ______________________________

4. ______________________________

5. ______________________________

Mark on the map the location of each rainforest.

VOLCANOES

Do some research, answer the questions, and write down some facts.

What is a volcano?

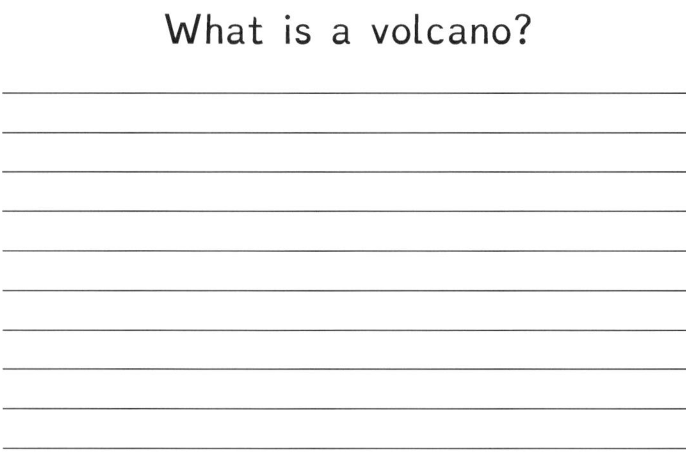

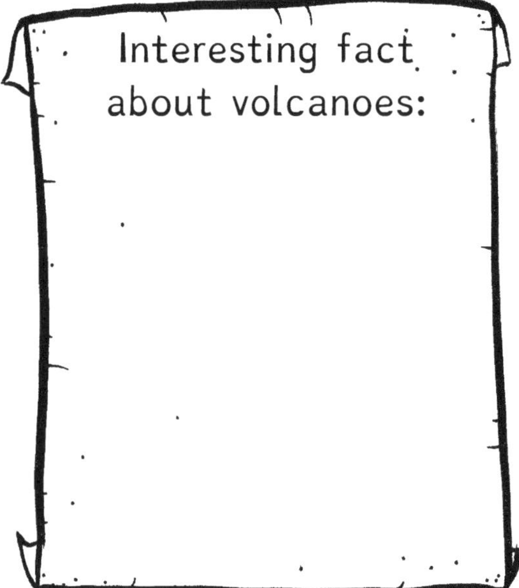

Fun fact about
volcanoes:

What is the largest active
volcano in the world?

What causes volcanoes to erupt?
Why are volcanoes so dangerous?

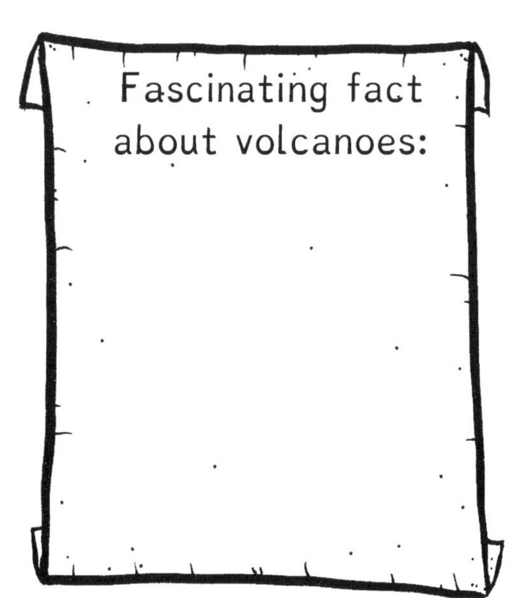

Draw some creatures, plants, and trees that could be found on a volcano.

Do some research, and answer the questions.

What is the current state of the closest volcano to you?

What kind of influence do people have on this environment?

How do people benefit from this environment?

Do some research, and list the top five most well-known volcanoes in the world. Write a short description for each one.

1. ______________________________

2. ______________________________

3. ______________________________

4. ______________________________

5. ______________________________

Mark on the map the location of each volcano.

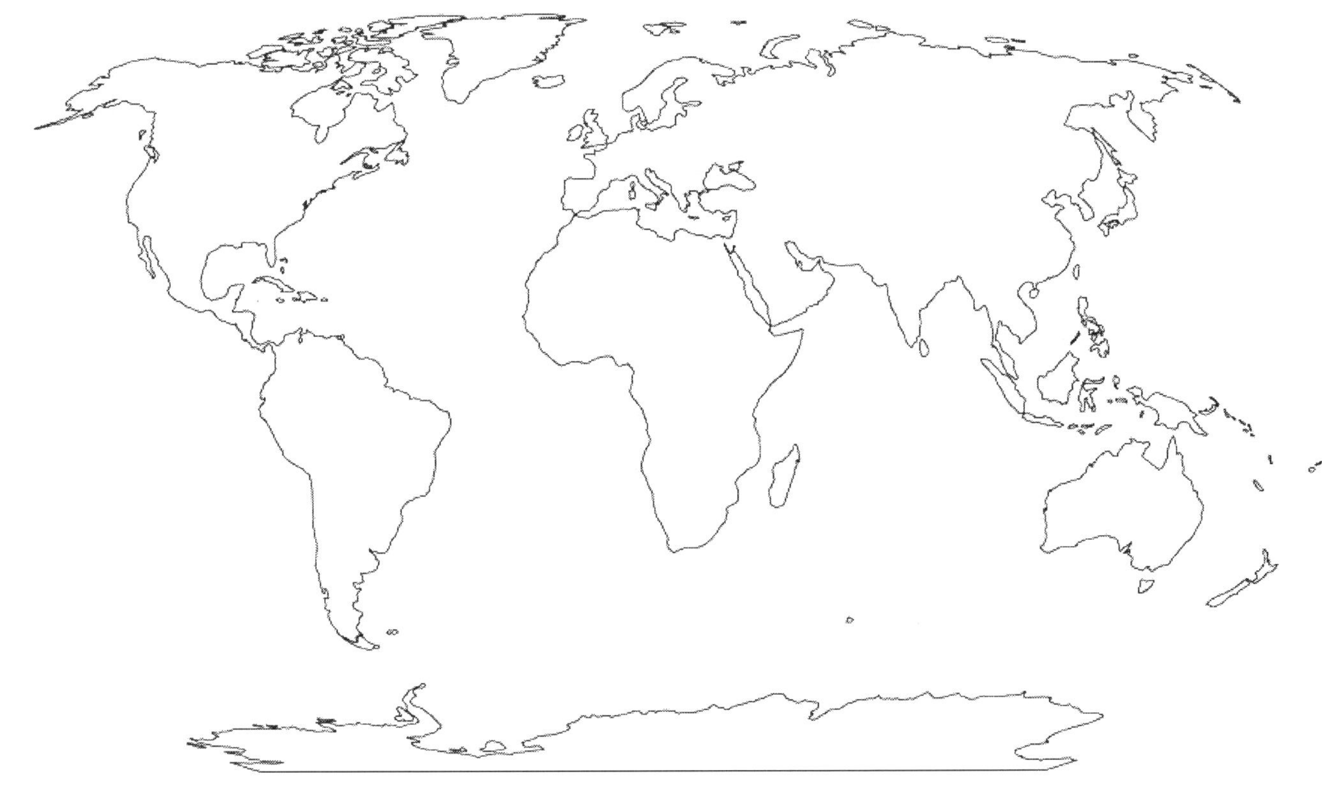

MOUNTAINS

Do some research, answer the questions, and write down three facts.

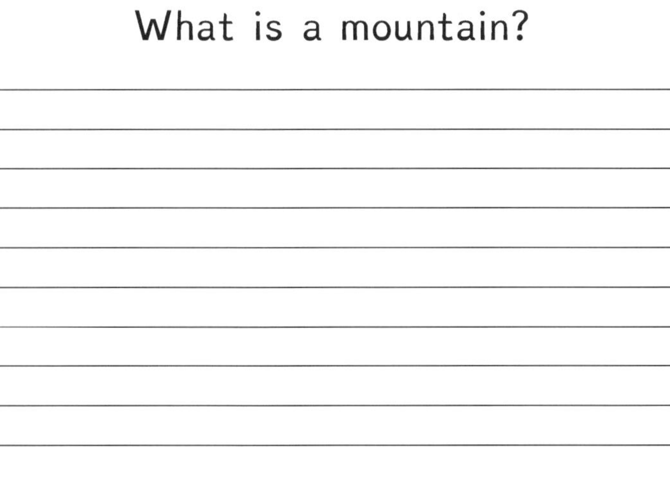

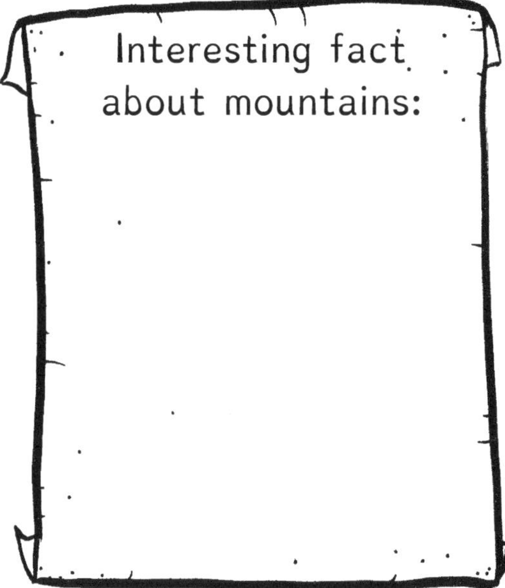

What are the different types of mountains?

What is the highest mountain in the world? What is its height?

Draw some creatures, plants, and trees that could be found on a mountain.

Do some research, and answer the questions.

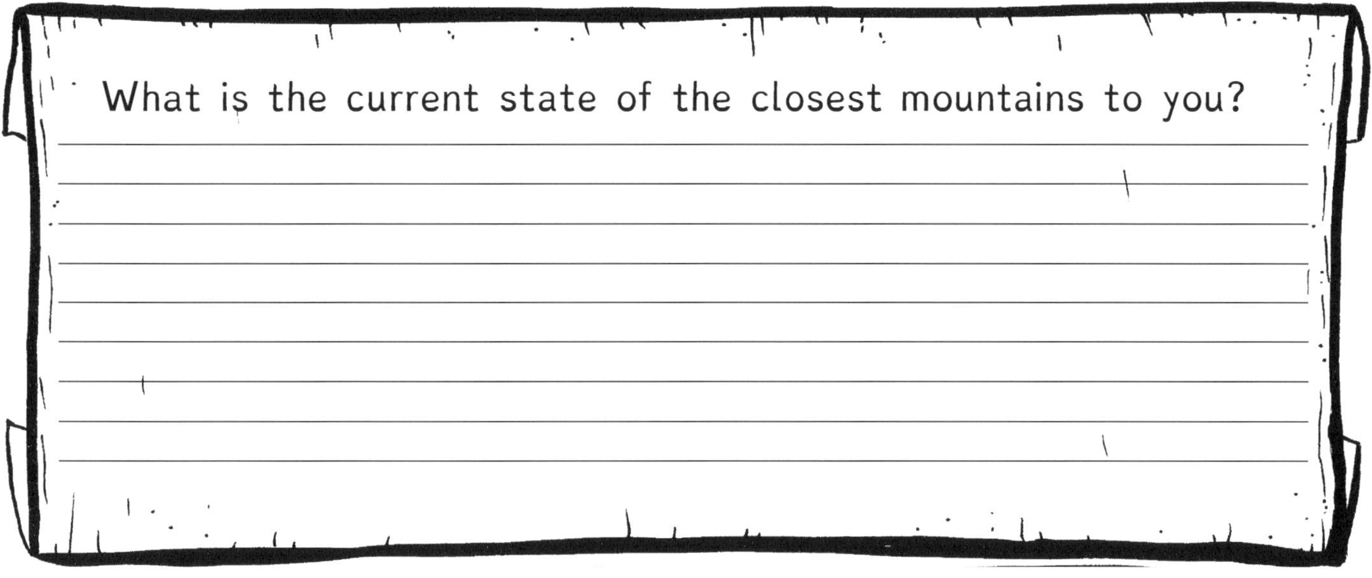

How do people benefit from this environment?

Do some research, and list the top five most well-known mountains in the world. Write a short description for each one.

1. ______________________________

2. ______________________________

3. ______________________________

4. ______________________________

5. ______________________________

Mark on the map the location of each mountain.

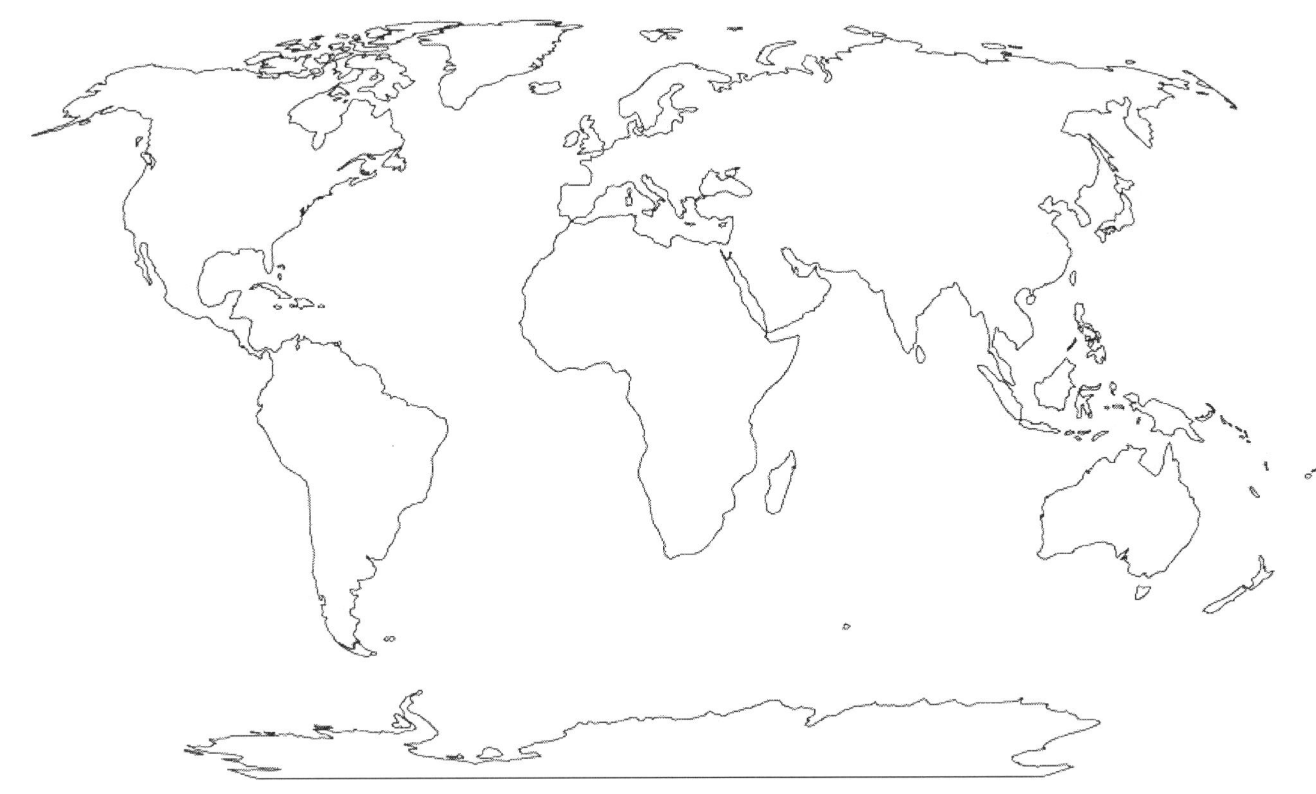

ICEBERGS

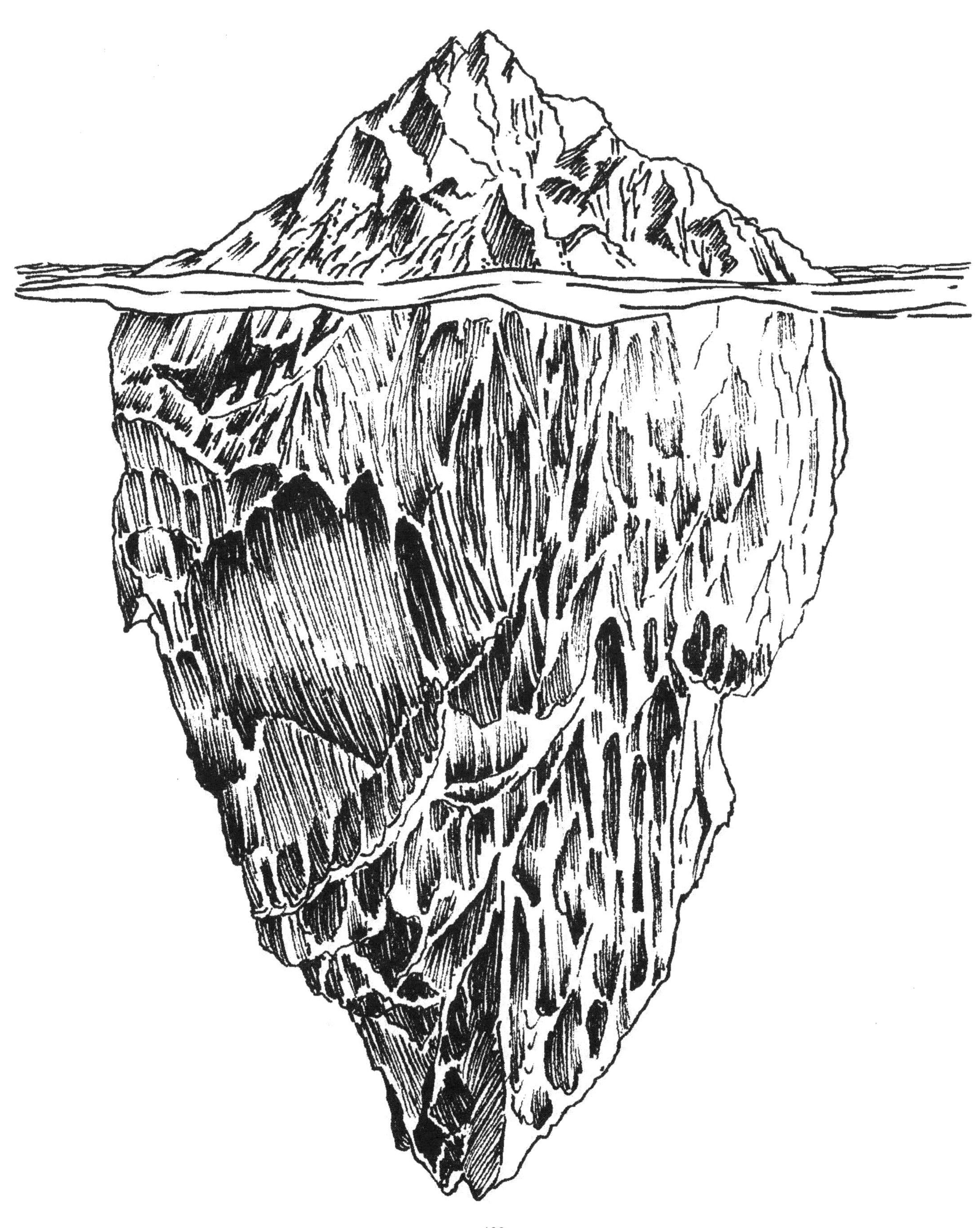

Do some research, answer the questions, and write down three facts.

What is an iceberg?

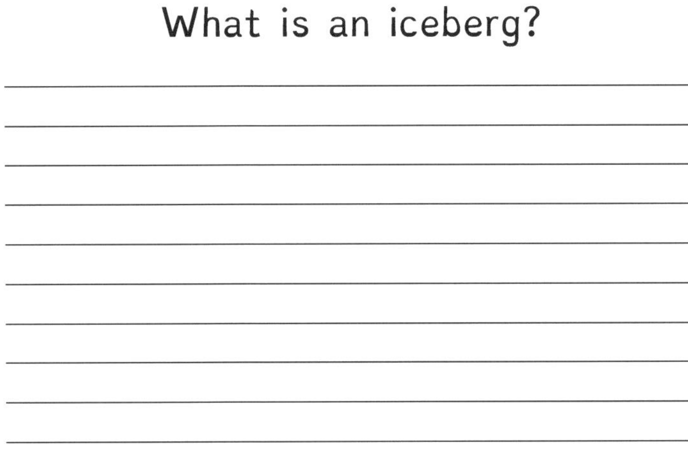

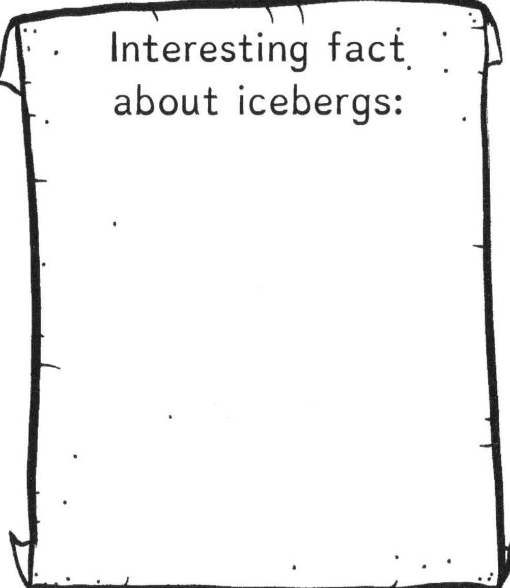

Fun fact about icebergs:

How do icebergs form?

What is the largest iceberg in the world? How deep does it go?

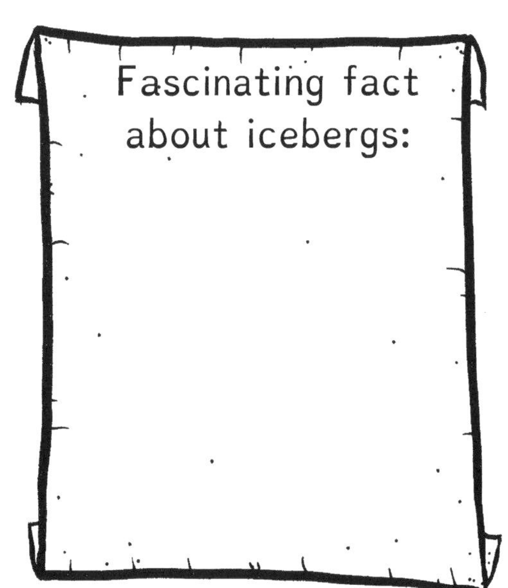

Do research about the different types of icebergs,
and try drawing one for yourself!

Do some research, and answer the questions.

What is the current state of the closest iceberg to you?

What kind of influence do people have on icebergs?

How do people benefit from icebergs?

Do some research, and list the top five most well-known icebergs in the world. Write a short description for each one.

1. ______________________________

2. ______________________________

3. ______________________________

4. ______________________________

5. ______________________________

Mark on the map the location of each iceberg.

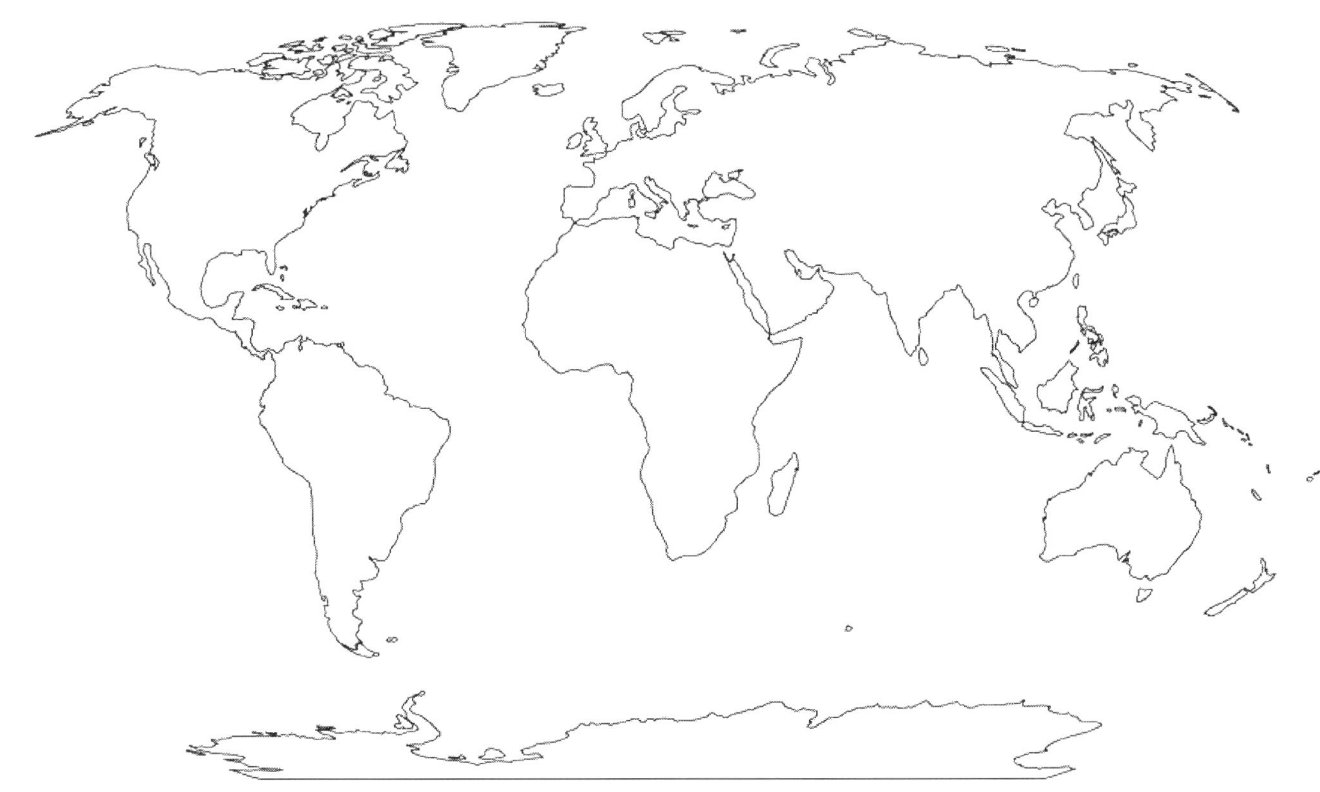

CRATERS

Do some research, answer the questions, and write down three facts.

What is a crater?

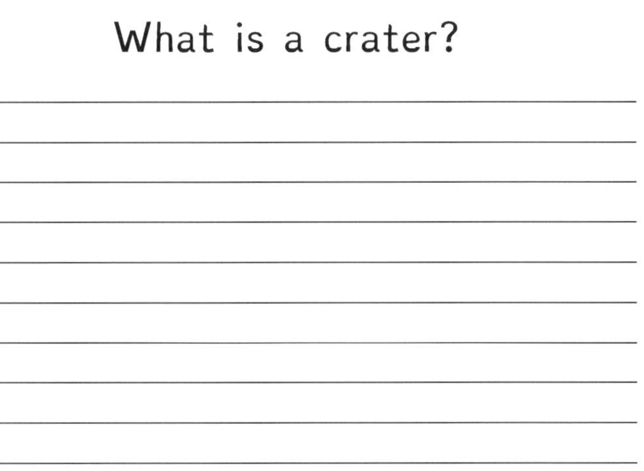

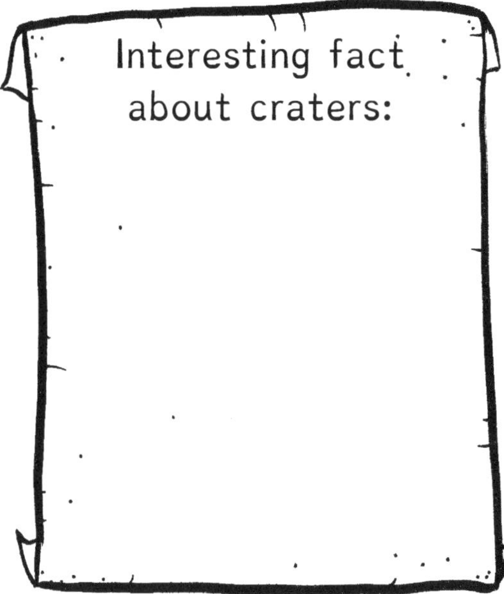

What are the different types of craters?

How do craters form?

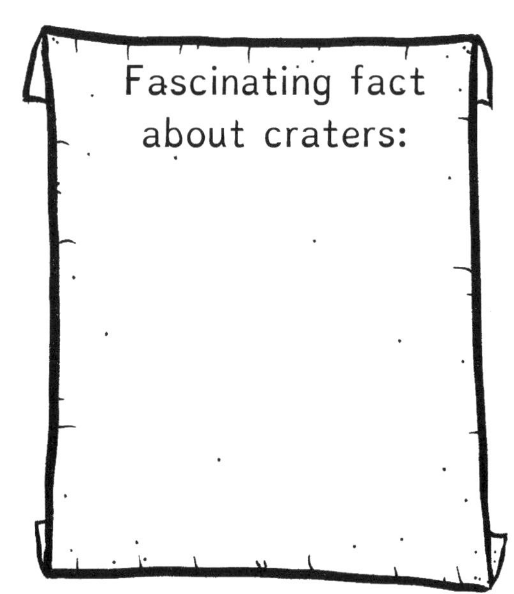

Do research about the different types of craters,
and try drawing one for yourself!

Do some research, and answer the questions.

What crater is the newest one on Earth? What is the story?

What kind of influence do people have on craters?

How do people benefit from craters?

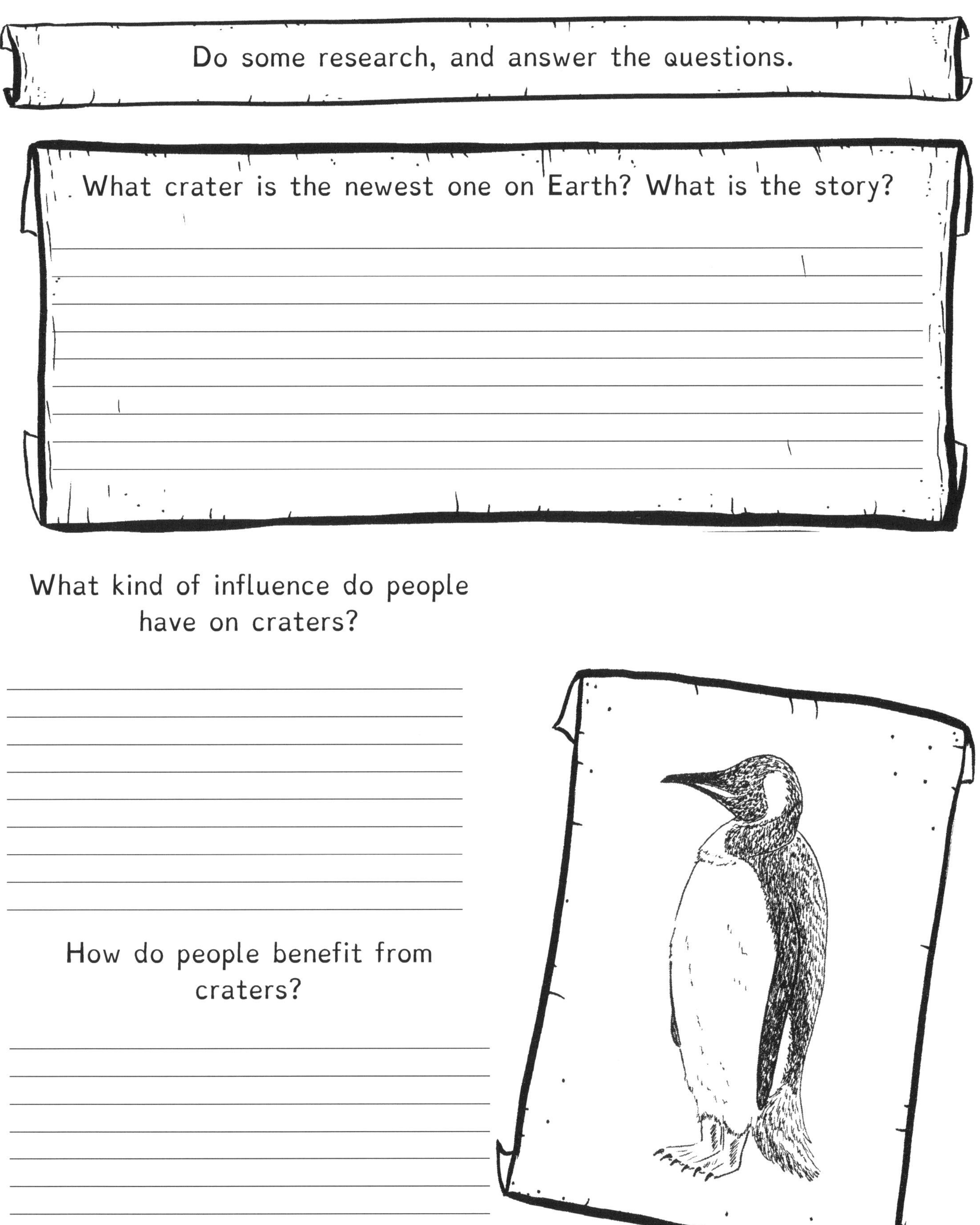

Do some research, and list the top five most well-known craters in the world. Write a short description for each one.

1. ______________________________

2. ______________________________

3. ______________________________

4. ______________________________

5. ______________________________

Mark on the map the location of each crater.

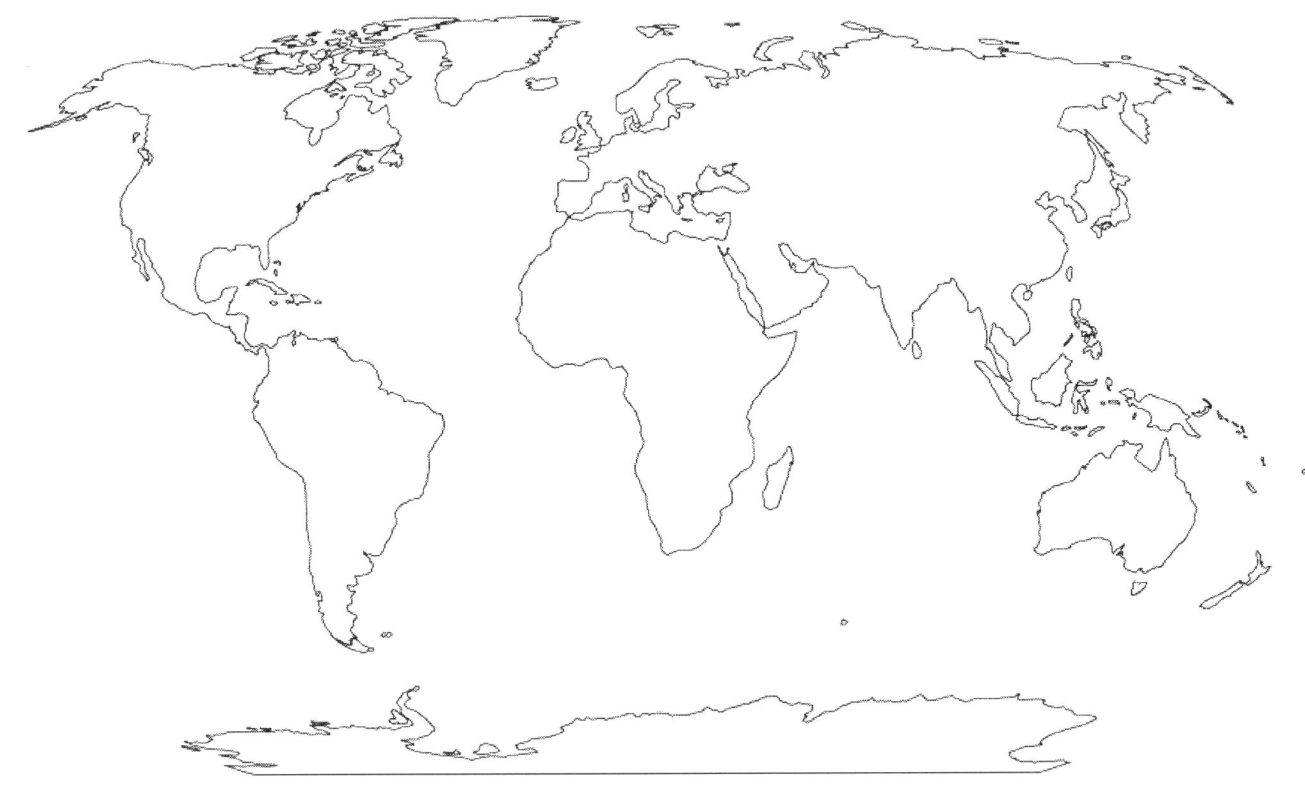

TUNDRA

Do some research, answer the questions, and write down three facts.

What is a tundra?

Interesting fact about tundra:

Fun fact about tundra:

What are the different types of tundras?

What climate does a tundra have?

Fascinating fact about tundra:

Draw some creatures, plants, and trees that could be found in a tundra.

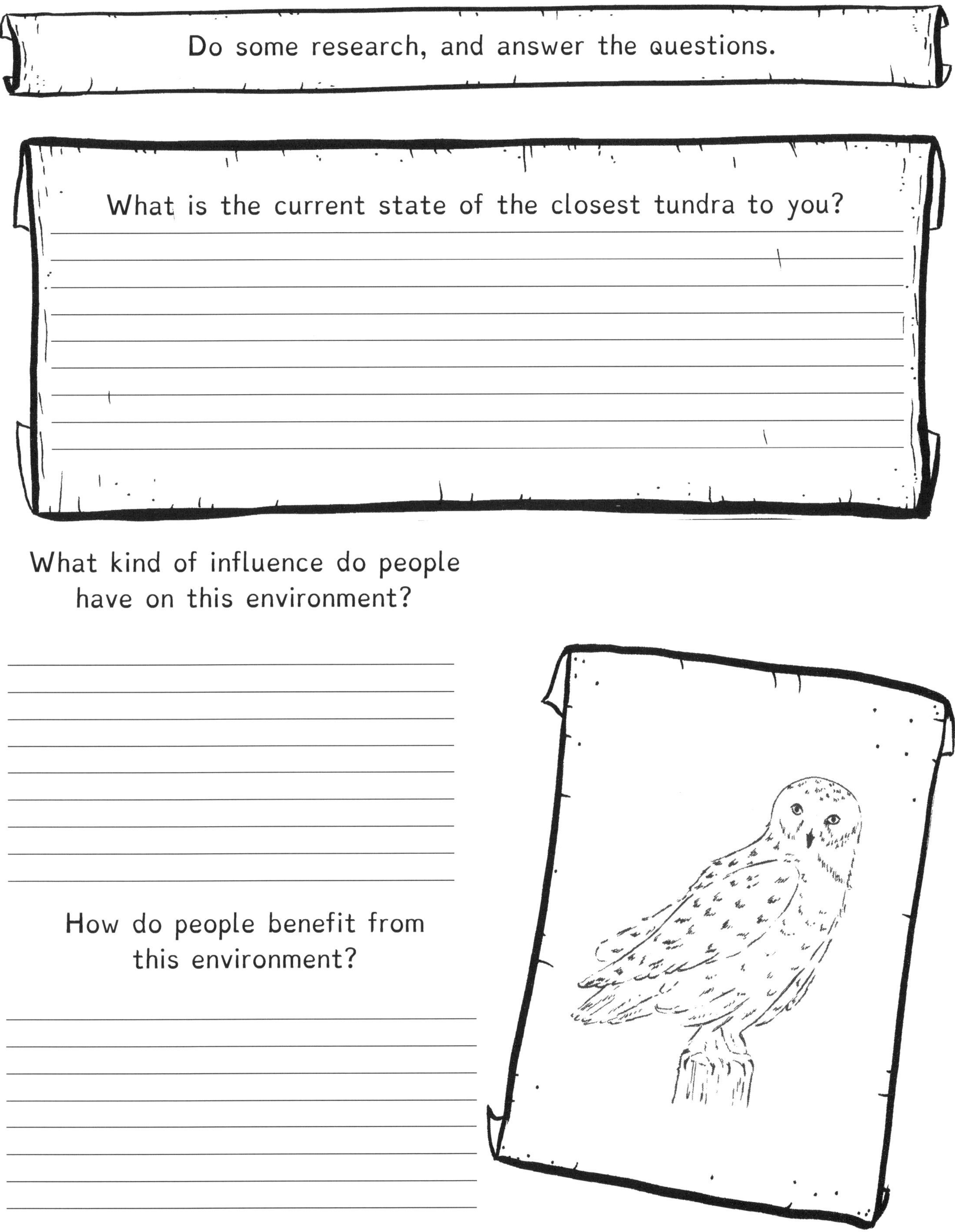

Do some research, and answer the questions.

What is the current state of the closest tundra to you?

What kind of influence do people have on this environment?

How do people benefit from this environment?

Do some research, and list the top five most well-known tundras in the world. Write a short description for each one.

1. ______________________________

2. ______________________________

3. ______________________________

4. ______________________________

5. ______________________________

Mark on the map the location of each tundra.

SWAMPS

Do some research, answer the questions, and write down three facts.

What is a swamp?

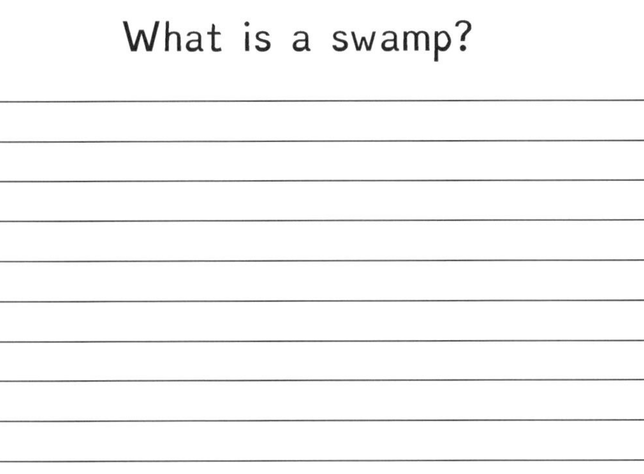

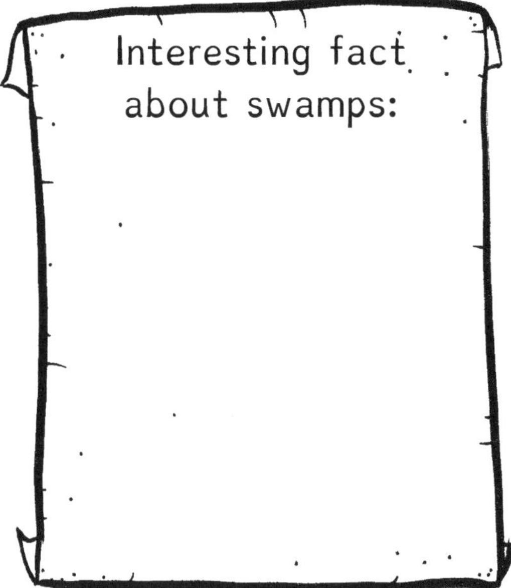

Interesting fact about swamps:

Fun fact about swamps:

What are the different types of swamps?

How do swamps form?

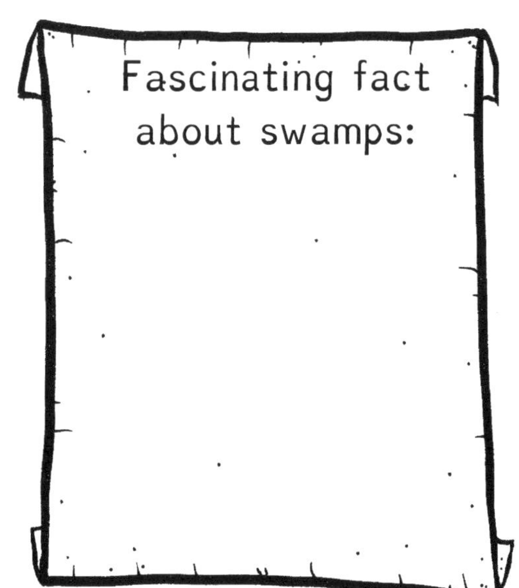

Fascinating fact about swamps:

Draw some creatures, plants, and trees that could be found in a swamp.

Do some research, and answer the questions.

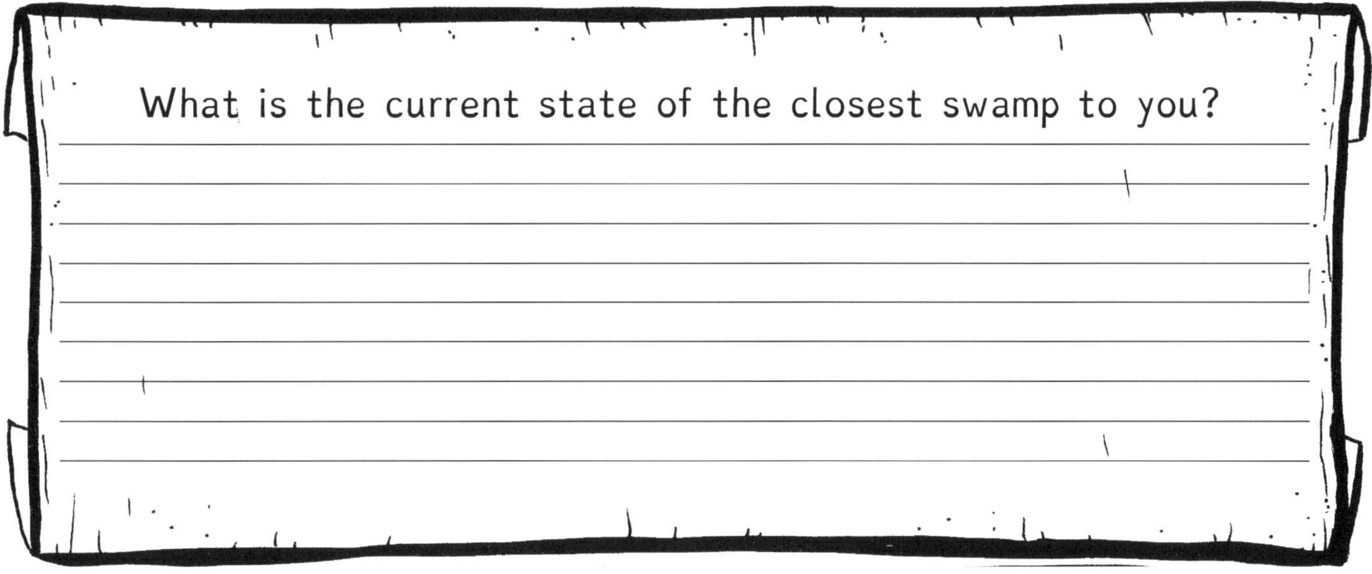

What is the current state of the closest swamp to you?

What kind of influence do people have on this environment?

How do people benefit from this environment?

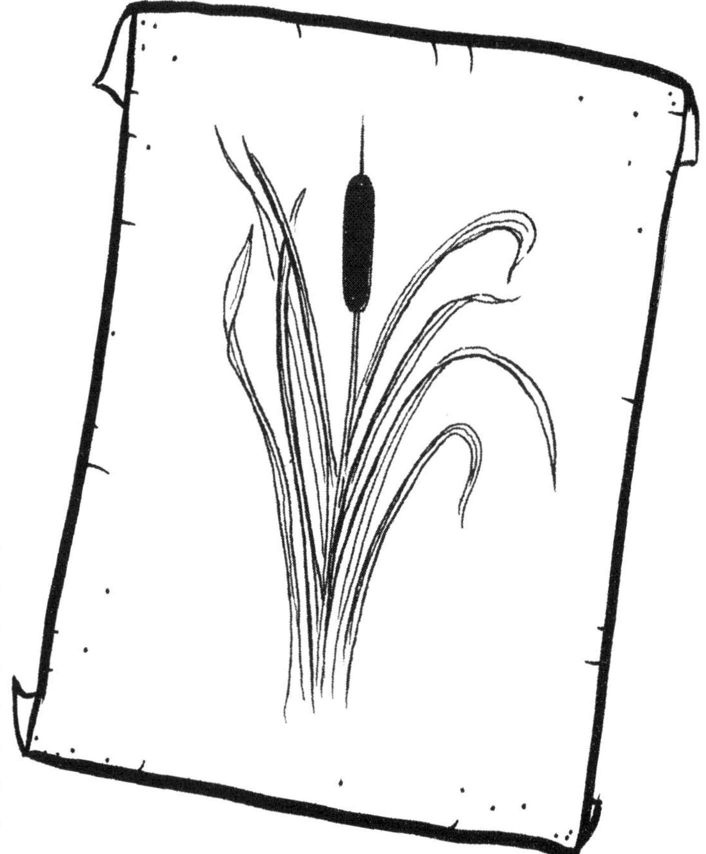

Do some research, and list the top five most well-known swamps in the world. Write a short description for each one.

1. ______________________________

2. ______________________________

3. ______________________________

4. ______________________________

5. ______________________________

Mark on the map the location of each swamp.

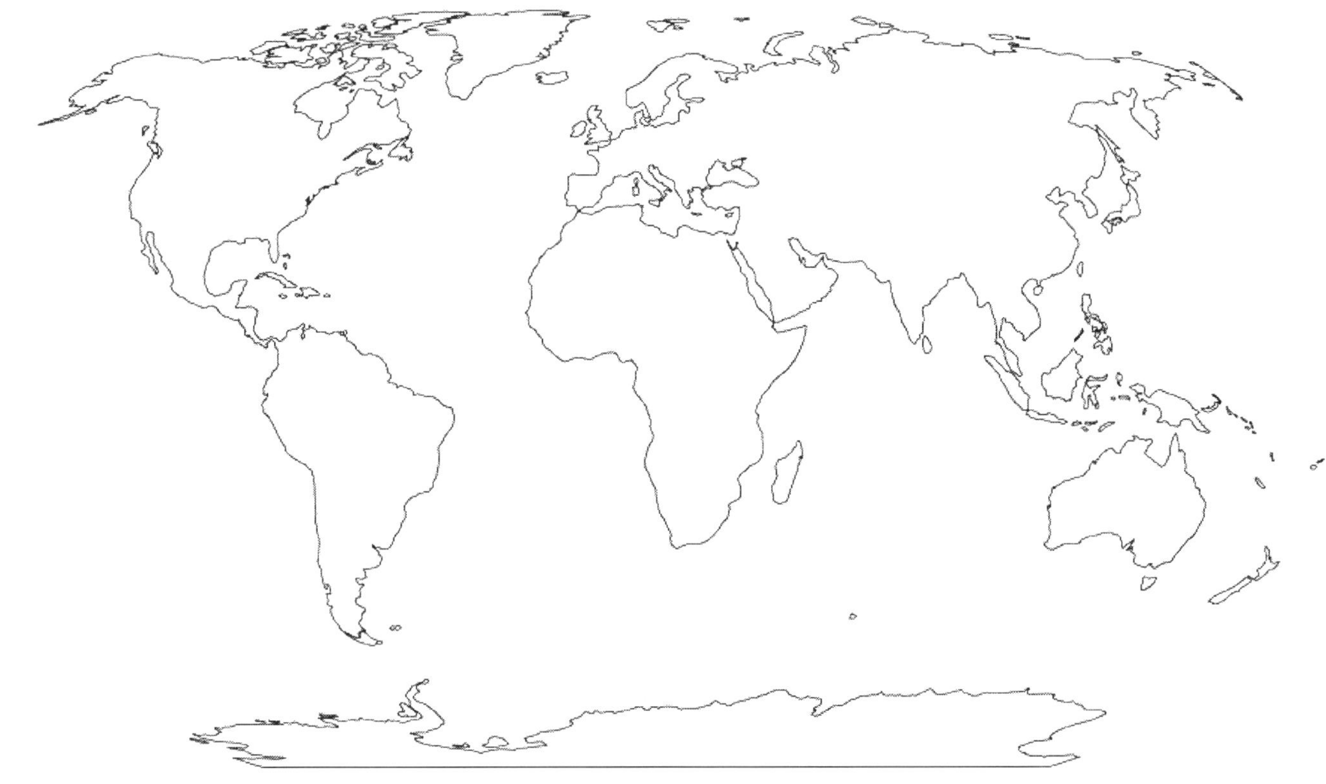

VALLEYS

Do some research, answer the questions, and write down some facts.

What is a valley?

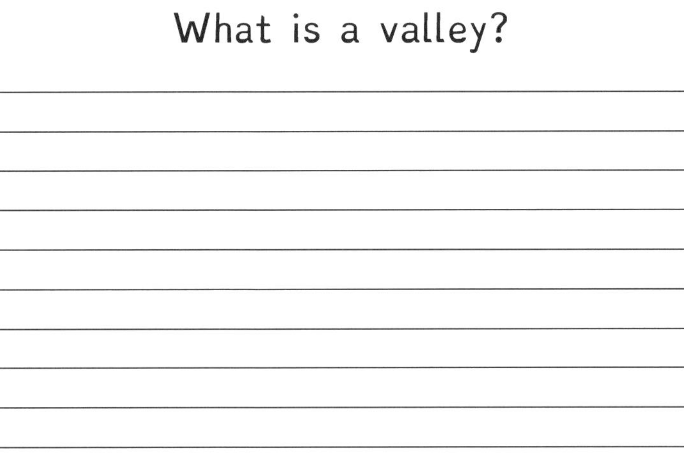

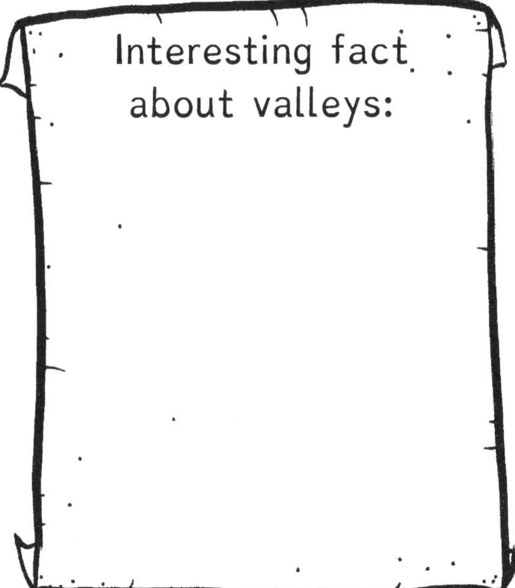

How do valleys form?

What are the different types of valleys?

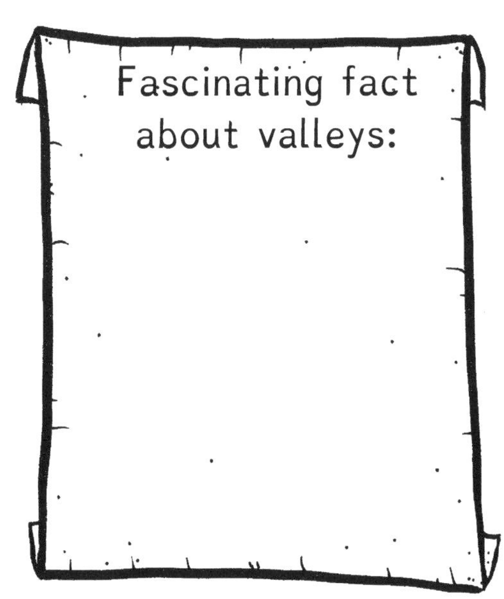

Draw some creatures, plants, and trees that could be found in or around a valley.

Do some research, and answer the questions.

What is the current state of the closest valley to you?

What kind of influence do people have on this environment?

How do people benefit from this environment?

Do some research, and list the top five most well-known valleys in the world. Write a short description for each one.

1. ____

2. ____

3. ____

4. ____

5. ____

Mark on the map the location of each valley.

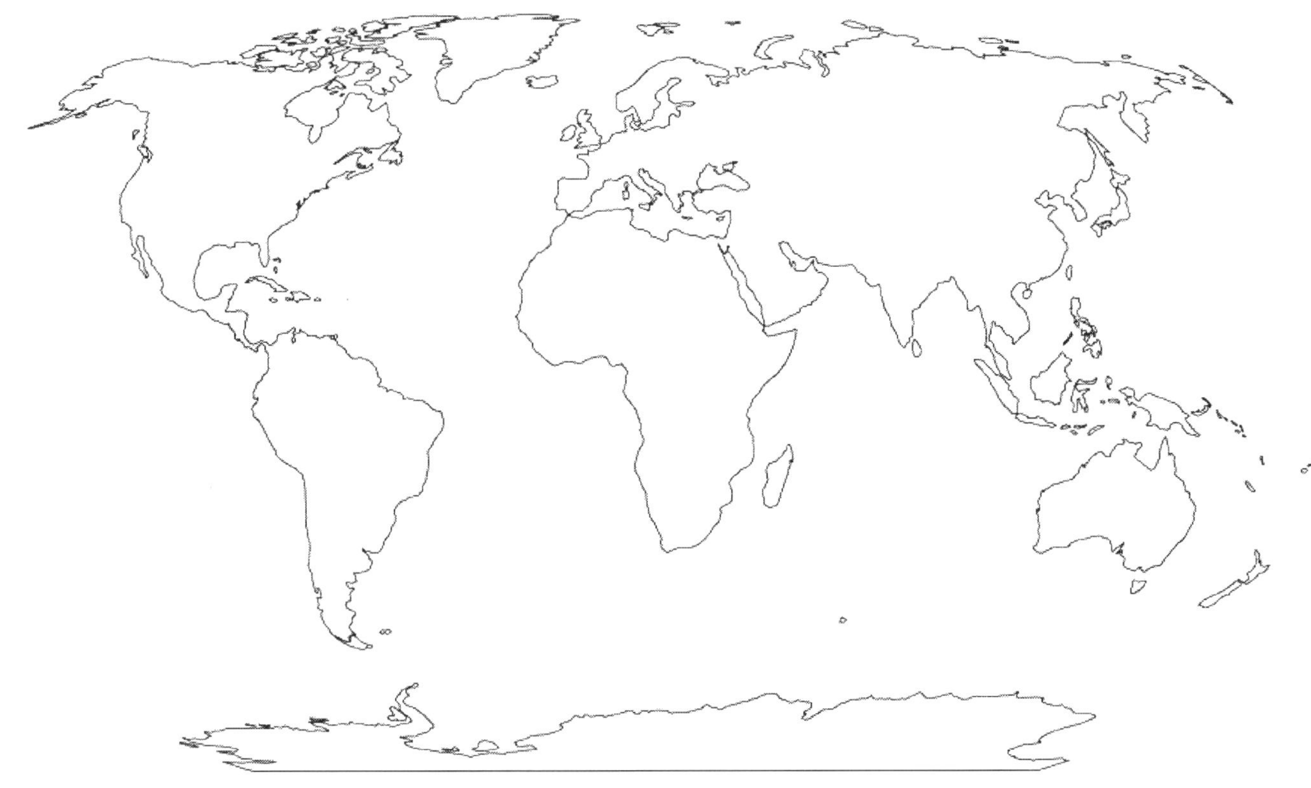

MEADOWS

Do some research, answer the questions, and write down three facts.

What is a meadow?

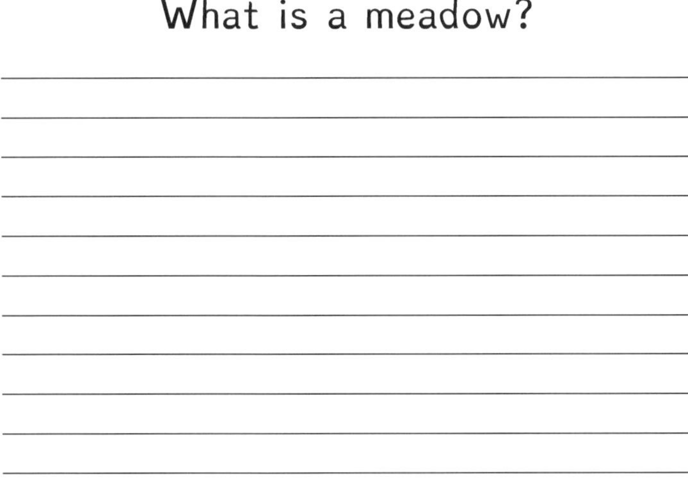

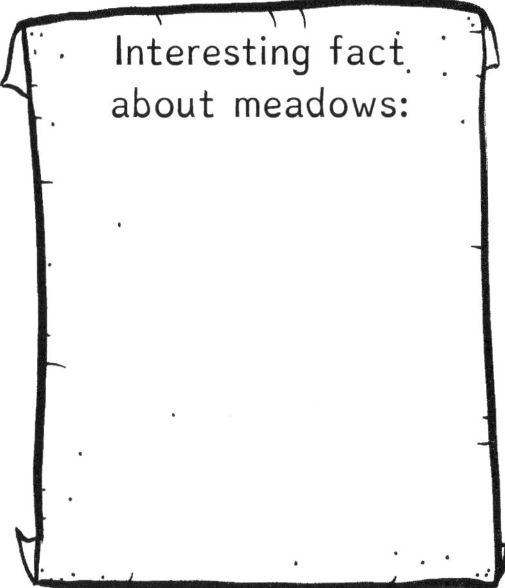

What are the different types of meadows?

What is the world's largest meadow?

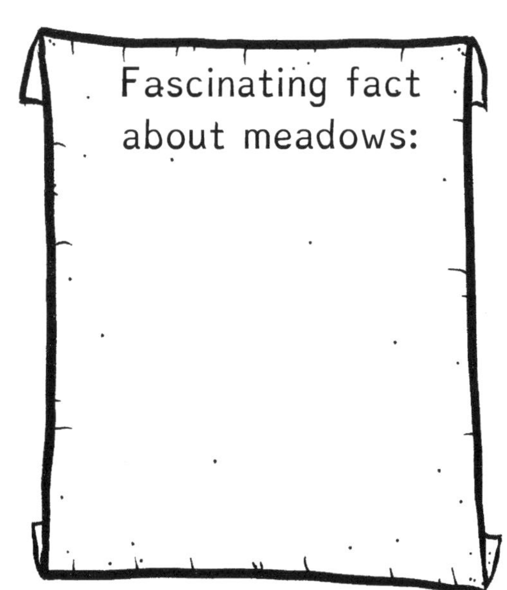

Draw some creatures, plants, and trees that could be found in a meadow.

Do some research, and answer the questions.

What is the current state of the closest meadow to you?

What kind of influence do people have on this environment?

How do people benefit from this environment?

HILLS

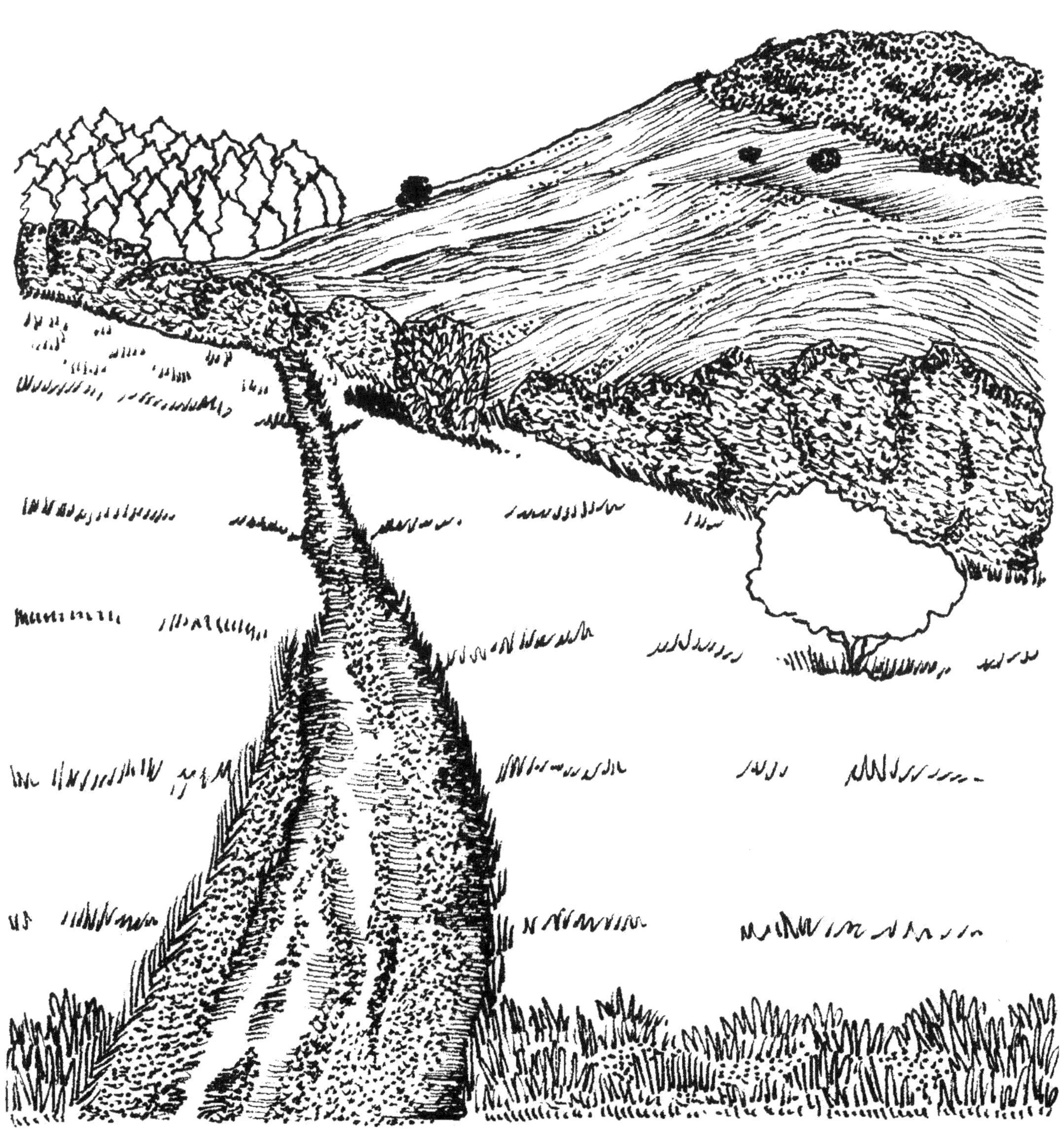

Do some research, answer the questions, and write down three facts.

What is a hill?

Interesting fact about hills:

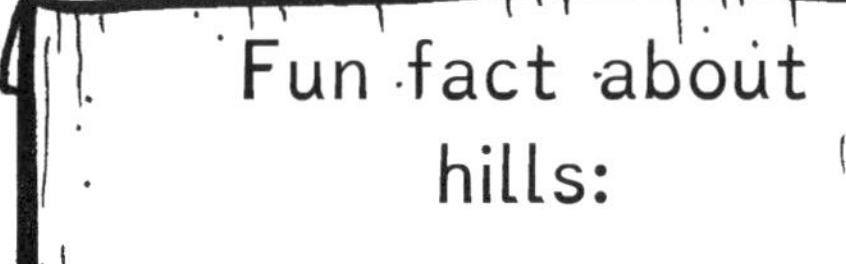

Fun fact about hills:

How are hills formed?

What is the difference between hills and mountains?

Fascinating fact about hills:

Draw some creatures, plants, and trees that could be found on a hill.

Do some research, and answer the questions.

What is the current state of the closest hill to you?

What kind of influence do people have on this environment?

How do people benefit from this environment?

CAVES

Do some research, answer the questions, and write down some facts.

What is a cave?

Interesting fact about caves:

Fun fact about caves:

What are the different types of caves?

How do caves form?

Fascinating fact about caves:

Draw some creatures, plants and formations
that could be found in a cave.

Do some research, and answer the questions.

What is the current state of the closest cave to you?

What kind of influence do people have on this environment?

How do people benefit from this environment?

Do some research, and list the top five most well-known caves in the world. Write a short description for each one.

1. ______________________________

2. ______________________________

3. ______________________________

4. ______________________________

5. ______________________________

Mark on the map the location of each cave.

SPRINGS

Do some research, answer the questions, and write down three facts.

What is a spring?

Interesting fact about springs:

Fun fact about springs:

What are the different types of springs?

How are springs formed?

Fascinating fact about springs:

Draw some creatures, plants, and trees that could be found in or around a spring.

Do some research, and answer the questions.

What is the current state of the closest spring to you?

What kind of influence do people have on this environment?

How do people benefit from this environment?

QUARRIES

Do some research, answer the questions, and write down three facts.

What is a quarry?

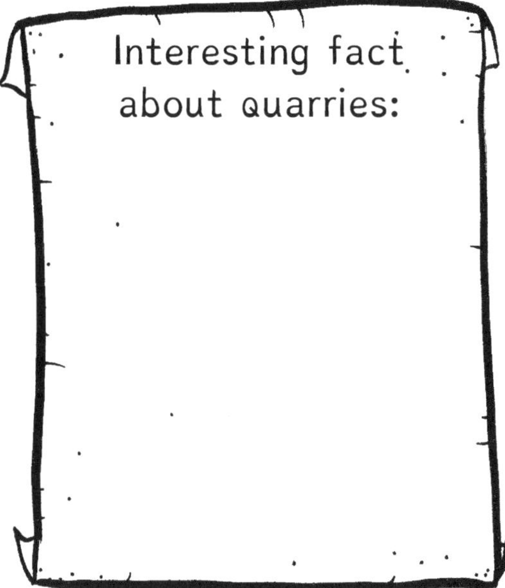

How are quarries formed? What are the different types of mines?

What is the largest quarry in the world?

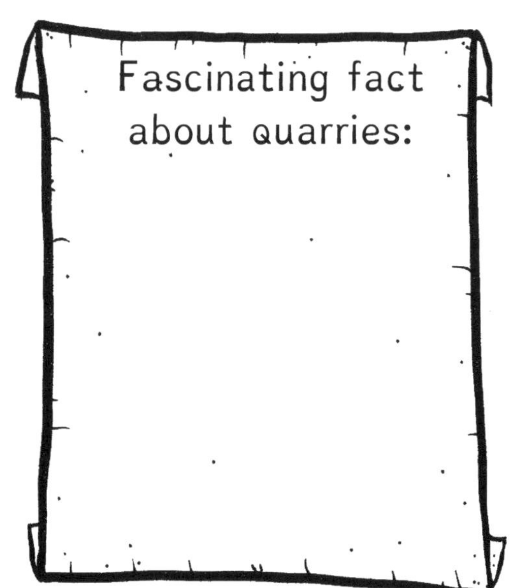

Draw some creatures, plants, and trees that could be found in or around a quarry.

Do some research, and answer the questions.

What is the current state of the closest spring to you?

What kind of influence do people have on this environment?

How do people benefit from this environment?

GLOSSARY

Savanna or **savannah:** a grassy plain in tropical and subtropical regions, with few trees, and bushes that are widely scattered.
Example: East Africa Plains.

River: a natural flowing stream of water, usually fresh water, flowing on the surface or inside caves into a sea, lake or another body of water.
Example: the Amazon in South America.

Lake: a large naturally occurring body of water completely surrounded by land.
Example: Lake Superior in North America.

Ocean: a large body of saltwater that fills the space between continents, and covers approximately 70.8% of the Earth, and contains 97% of Earth's water.
Example: Pacific Ocean.

Sea: a body of saltwater smaller than an ocean but greater than a lake or river.
Example: the Mediterranean Sea.

Waterfall: a cascade of water falling from a height, formed when a river or a stream flows over a vertical drop or a series of steep drops.
Example: Sutherland Falls in New Zealand.

Forest: an area of land dominated by trees and covered with undergrowth.
Example: Tongass National Forest in Alaska.

Lagoon: a shallow body of water separated from a larger body of water by narrow landform such as sandbars, barrier peninsulas, barrier islands, or coral reef.
Example: The lagoon of Bora Bora in French Polynesia.

Desert: any large, extremely dry and barren area of land where living conditions are hostile for most plants and animals.
Example: the Sahara Desert in Africa.

Glacier: a slowly moving large mass of ice formed by the accumulation and compaction of snow on mountains or near the poles.
Example: the Vatnajokull Glacier in Iceland.

Pond: a small body of still water, usually smaller than a lake, formed naturally or artificially.
Example: a backyard garden pond.

Stream: a small and narrow body of running water that flows into a river.

Canyon: a deep narrow valley, typically with a river flowing throw it with steep sides.
Example: the Grand Canyon in the United States.

Island: a landmass completely surrounded by water.
Example: Hawaii in the Pacific Ocean.

Plateau: also called a high plain or a tableland, is an area of a highland consisting of flat terrain that is raised sharply above the surrounding area on at least one side.
Example: the Tibetan Plateau in Asia.

Hot spring: also called hydrothermal spring, or geothermal spring is a spring produced by the emergence of geothermally heated groundwater onto the surface of the Earth. The groundwater is heated either by shallow bodies of magma or by circulation through faults to hot rock deep in the Earth's crust.
Example: the geothermal pools in Yellowstone National Park in the United States.

Plain: also called flatland, is a flat expanse of land that generally does not change much in elevation, and is primarily treeless. Plains occur as lowlands along valleys, or at the base of mountains, as coastal plains, and as plateaus or uplands.
Example: the Great Plains in North America.

Oasis: a fertile area of a desert or semi-desert environment that sustains plant life and provides habitat for animals. Surface water may be present, or water may only be accessible from wells or underground channels created by humans.
Example: Huacachina Oasis, Peru.

Geyser: a hot spring characterized by an intermittent discharge of water ejected turbulently and accompanied by steam. As a fairly rare phenomenon, the formation of geysers is due to particular hydrogeological conditions that exist only in a few places on Earth.
Example: Old Faithful in Yellowstone National Park in the United States.

Rainforest: a dense forest that is typically found in tropical areas with consistently heavy rainfall.
Example: the Amazon Rainforest in South America

Volcano: an opening in the Earth's crust through which lava, ash, and gases erupt.
Example: Mount Vesuvius, Italy.

Mountain: a large natural elevation of the Earth's surface.
Example: the Alps, Europe.

Iceberg: a large floating mass of ice that has broken off a glacier or an ice shelf and is floating freely in open water.
Example: Iceberg B15

Crater: a landform consisting of a hole or depression on a planetary surface, usually caused either by an object like meteor hitting the surface, or volcano or explosion.
Example: Meteor Crater Northern Arizona in the United States

Tundra: a biome where tree growth is hindered by frigid temperatures and short growing seasons.
Example: Canadian Arctic Tundra

Swamp: a wetland areas with standing water and trees.
Example: the Okefenokee Swamp in the United States.

Valley: a depressed area of land between hills and mountains.
Example: Valley of the Ten Peaks, Canada

Meadow: an open field of grass, herbs, and wildflowers.
Example: a meadow in the English countryside.

Hill: a natural elevation of the Earth's surface, smaller than a mountain.
Example: the Hollywood Hills in California, United States.

Quarry: a place, typically a large, deep pit, from which stone or other materials are or have been extracted. A quarry is a type of mine called an open-pit mine, because it is open to the Earth's surface.
Example: Marble Quarry in Carrara Tuscany, Italy.

THE Thinking TREE
PUBLISHING COMPANY
ART
LOGIC
SCIENCE
SPELLING
READING
COLORING
THINKING
DRAWING
CREATING
Sarah Janisse Brown